CONTENTS

CORO T
EXTRAORDINARY LANDSCAPES

Vincent Pomarède and Gérard de Wallens

Translated from the French by Lisa Davidson

DÉCOUVERTES GALLIMARD
RÉUNION DES MUSÉES NATIONAUX
PAINTING

Corot has been considered many things: a precursor of Impressionism, with his sophisticated play of light in morning fog; a Romantic, for the lyricism in his landscapes; a Realist, for painting directly from nature; and a Neoclassicist by training. Yet ultimately, was he the last of the classical landscape painters or the first poet to praise the simple beauties of nature?

CHAPTER ONE
THE UNEVENTFUL CHILDHOOD OF A FUTURE CLOTH MERCHANT

Corot's intent observation of the postures of the female body began in "the rendezvous of the Graces," as he called the family business. By 1817, the region around Ville-d'Avray, particularly the towns of Sèvres and Chaville, replaced Paris in the imagination of the young painter (left, detail of *Little Chaville*).

Jean-Baptiste Camille Corot's childhood was not that of a prodigy, and he displayed no particular interest in the arts in adolescence. His love of painting and drawing did not appear until the age of 19, and he only began his career when he was 26 years old. He exhibited for the first time in the Salon of 1827, when he was 31. He clearly did not welcome spectacular events or dramatic developments, preferring instead a slow and deliberate process of maturation. His work, which revolved around three

Corot attempted his first subject on the banks of the Seine near his mother's store, which was located on the first floor of an elegant building. He frequented this neighborhood until the 1850s, as he had a studio at 15, quai Voltaire.

or four main themes—subjects that were constantly elaborated and enriched in admirable variations—reflects this part of his personality well.

Corot's parents: "dignified and formal" merchants

The success of the Corot family in the fashion world stemmed from their clothing and millinery shop located in Paris on the corner of the rue de Bac and the quai Voltaire, opposite the Pont-Royal. His mother, whose maiden name was Marie-Françoise Oberson (1768–1851), was an orphan; sometime around 1798 she used her inheritance to purchase the clothing store that carried her name. Louis Jacques Corot (1771–1847), from Burgundy, devoted all his time to his wife's millinery business. She was the designer, while he managed the business, which became a well-known establishment during the Empire and Restoration. "One could encounter Mme de Colbert, Mme Kellermann,

"This hat was created by Madame Corot; no one else can fashion [a hat] like that," recorded the *Album ou journal des Arts, des Modes et de Théâtres,* which rented the models from her shop for their high-society clientele (right, invoice dated 1819 for supplies to the comtesse de Clermont-Tonnerre). An engraving by Gavarni, published around 1830—after Mme Corot had transferred management of the shop to her daughter Annette Octavie— is a testimony to her fame.

Rue du Bac, N.° 1 — en face le Pont Royal

Mme. COROT — Mde. de Modes

Madame la Duchesse d'Orléans,

Mademoiselle d'Orléans.

de Clermont tonnerre

blanche — 188

chapeau de paille fournie les ruban

une ruche de tul blanchie la paille — 35

chapeau de paille fournie les ruban

rosé et blanchie la paille — 20

deux chapeau de Velours Noir

fournie cinq plumes

avoir fait teindre cinq plum

un chapeau de pluche Noir

un chapeau de crêpe rose garnie d'

un chapeau de Velours Noir petit b

un chapeau de paille blan

un chapeau de Velours Violet

un bonnet blanc garnie de

fournie pour un chapeau

un chapeau de crêpe blan

un bonnet de tul et blon

un chapeau de Velours Epi

blanchi

Pour acquit pour solde. Paris le

Mme de Fitz-James or Mme Condorcet, depending on the items in the shop," wrote Étienne Moreau-Nélaton, one of Corot's most famous biographers. The family grew wealthy from this business, a situation augmented by various real estate investments.

Annette Octavie (1793–1874) was born shortly after their marriage. Jean-Baptiste Camille was next on July 16, 1796, at 1:30 A.M., followed by a second daughter, Victoire Anne (1797–1821), the year after.

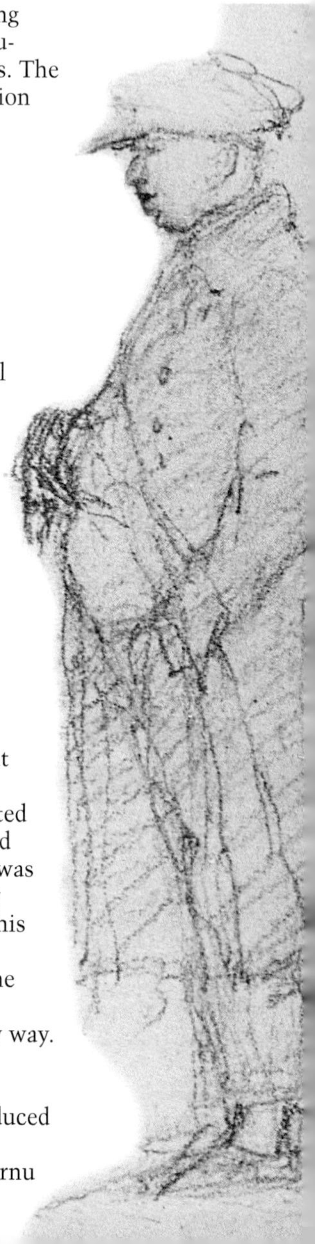

Well-to-do but dependent on his family

The comfortable financial situation of Corot's parents meant that he never experienced material difficulties in his career. "Without the well-supplied coffers of his father, farewell to the large canvases gathering dust on the walls of his studio, farewell to the disinterested apprenticeship in the forests of Fontainebleau," wrote Moreau-Nélaton. In exchange, however, he was deeply dependent on his family. Indeed, until the death of his mother in 1851, Corot still lived with his parents, owning nothing of his own. "They gave me enough to live on," he admitted candidly many years later. Yet it is disturbing to read in a letter written in 1849 to his friend Constant Dutilleux—when Corot was 53—that he could not travel to Arras without his mother's permission. Alfred Robaut, Corot's friend and confidant in his later years who collected documents concerning each of his works, reported that Corot regretted that "until the age of 40, he was treated as a grown-up child of limited capacity by parents he always worshipped." But Corot loved his parents too much to hold any bitterness against them, and although he often complained about the "chains" that left him "very little freedom," this situation did not adversely affect his career in any way.

"A calm, unremarkable life"

"There are very few examples… of a life that produced so many excellent works yet that developed so calmly and was so unremarkable," wrote Paul Cornu

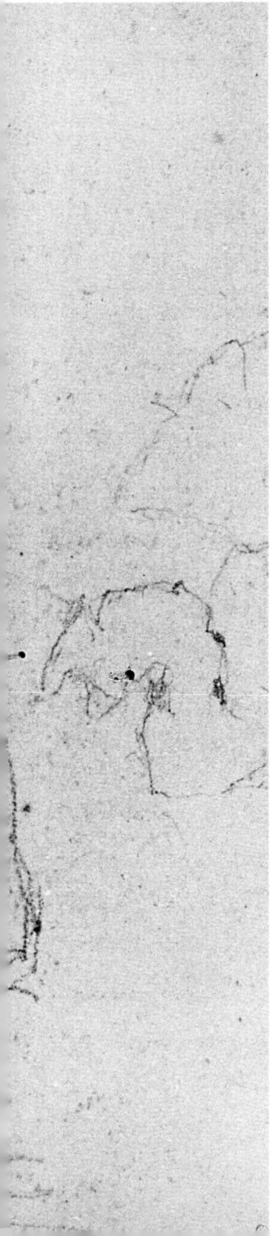

in 1911. Corot's parents were kept busy in their shop and had little time to take care of the children. Jean-Baptiste Camille was placed in the care of a nurse in Presles, a small village north of Paris near L'Isle-Adam. This was quite common at the time and the boy did not seem traumatized by this separation, any more than when he entered boarding school on the rue de Vaugirard in Paris at the age of four.

In 1807 Corot's father managed to obtain a scholarship for his son to attend the Collège de Rouen, where he stayed five years, until 1812. Despite his undistinguished school records, the years in Normandy had a decisive effect on Corot: he learned to love nature and took long walks in the countryside, a habit he enjoyed throughout his life.
A certain M. Sennegon, one of his father's friends, lived near Rouen in the small village of Bois-Guillaume. He became something of a second father to the boy, who spent Sundays and short vacations with the family. This kind-hearted man, had "fled from the world, but relished nature." Under his influence, Corot learned to appreciate the subtlety and power of nature, an experience that confirmed his future career as a painter. He had not yet started painting, but his

Louis Jacques Corot (left), who came from the region of Semur-en-Auxois in Burgundy, was the son of a wig-maker. Fatherless, he inherited the family business when he married in 1793; he immediately sold it to contribute his funds to the purchase of his wife's shop. Corot's father stubbornly opposed his son's repeated and obstinate requests—which began in 1815—to become a painter. Finally in 1822, his father agreed to finance his vocation without making any further conditions on his allowance; this assistance gave Corot the means to travel and buy the expensive materials he needed for the large works he submitted to the Salons. Corot was unable to support himself from selling paintings and until the day he finally received the Legion of Honor medal, in 1846, Louis Jacques Corot never believed his son would be a professional success. His mother, Marie-Françoise Corot, from Fribourg in Switzerland, was the daughter of a wine merchant who moved to Versailles during the Monarchy. Corot lived under the divided rule of his parents: his father controlled his financial situation, while his mother took care of his clothes and social life.

deep love of nature took root in this period. "In spring, when I smell the scent of the hazelnut trees, my imagination flies back to Bois-Guillaume, near Rouen, where I spent my childhood, and buries itself in the fragrant thickets where I used to wander on Sundays, collecting mushrooms," he told his first biographer, Théophile Silvestre, in 1853.

"My father dreamed I would be a successful businessman"

Corot completed his studies in a boarding school in Poissy and then began a series of apprenticeships with cloth merchants. The first was Ratier—who quickly discharged his rather absent-minded employee. Corot then spent the next five years working for Yves Delalain in a shop called "Le Calife de Bagdad."

Most art historians, eager to vaunt Corot's "genius," have consistently dismissed this period of his life, insisting on his "aversion to business." Yet these years as an apprentice cloth merchant left a mark on Corot's career: he formed a close circle of friends among the cloth merchants and businessmen, who were among the first to collect his works. He also met art dealers, and although his contacts with them were occasionally complicated, he well understood their professional point of view. He learned to love the beautiful textures of the fabrics he handled before starting his day. With these cloth merchants, who were often talented cloth dyers as well, Corot began to understand the secrets of color harmony. Later on, he discussed the similarity of the techniques used by painters and dyers, telling Théophile Silvestre that "fabric designers are almost always able to match their colors."

It was around this time that Corot was drawn to painting and attempted his first oil on canvas. Without his parent's knowledge, he bought a set of paints, but was found out when he ruined good pieces of fabric with spots of oil. He probably sneaked away to draw from the model at the

"Life alone attracts and captivates him. He turns his back on the masterpieces to draw the copyists at their easels." Moreau-Nélaton's comments on a drawing (below) are meant to support the myth that Corot did not like to copy the masters, that he rarely went to the Louvre, and that he was even scolded by the guards one day for particularly rowdy behavior.

"When I finished at the *lycée,* my father sent me to one of his friends, an important cloth merchant in the Bourdonnais

neighborhood near Les Halles. Naturally, the first rule I was taught was to sell —honestly—inferior goods for the best possible price to those who didn't know any better."
Corot to Armand Leleux

Académie Suisse, a famous private school set up at 4, quai des Orfèvres by one of Louis Jacques David's former models. In 1815, when he dared reveal his desire to become a painter, his father "laughed in his face." For years he received the same reaction every time he repeated his request.

A painter at last!

Corot had to wait until early 1822, just a few months after his sister Victoire Anne died, before his father finally offered him a choice: he could receive his share of the inheritance—about 100,000 francs—to set up his own cloth business, or he could receive an annual

At Bois-Guillaume near Rouen, Corot selected subjects from nature, not because they were picturesque or poetic, but to learn to work realistically. When he painted the entrance gate to the Sennegons' property (above) he was only interested in the reflections of the light on the stone of the posts, on the dirt path, and on the leaves and tree trunks.

Sketched in a notebook (left), the portrait of Mme Delalain, the wife of his second employer in the cloth trade.

allowance of 1,500 to 2,000 francs, and live as he chose, without touching the capital. "That night I told my father that business and I were simply incompatible, and that I was getting a divorce!" At the age of 26, Corot finally began to paint in earnest.

"So, I'm an artist," he repeated to himself as he wandered through the streets, still undecided over his next step. Then in the spring of 1822, he enrolled in the studio of Achille Etna Michallon (1796–1822), one of David's former protégés and the most promising landscape artist of his generation.

Neoclassical training

He discovered the fundamentals of his craft with Michallon, who convincingly transmitted his love of Neoclassical landscapes, an ideal defended by its major theorist, Pierre Henri de Valenciennes (1750–1819).

Achille Etna Michallon (left) was the son of a sculptor who died during the French Revolution. As a child, he benefited from the protection of the painter David and other wealthy patrons. He learned the classical tradition of landscape painting by attending the studios of the great masters of his time (Valenciennes, Dunouy and Bertin). In 1817, when the Prix de Rome was created for historical landscape painting, he was the first to receive the award, for a work painted in the manner of Poussin: *Democritus and the Abderites.* He stayed at the Villa Medici in Rome from 1818 to 1821 and painted open-air studies to prepare the historical compositions sent to the Salons. By the time he returned to Paris, the Restoration had replaced the Empire. In 1815, Michallon no longer enjoyed the support of his former patrons and for financial reasons, opened a studio in Paris. Among his first students were Corot, Antoine Guindrand and Léon Fleury, who became close friends.

Although steeped in classical tradition, Michallon was able to integrate the northern style of landscape painting, as in his drawing *Oak and Reed,* inspired from one of La Fontaine's fables.

Under Michallon's guidance, Corot copied antique sculptures, and works by Renaissance masters and the great seventeenth-century landscapists. Michallon also gave Corot some of his own open-air studies to copy: views of Italy, Paris and Normandy. But his education was not limited to copies. "Our student has... copied several paintings by several masters, but he has not seen Nature," said Valenciennes. "He needs it as a reference, and when it gets nice, we will go together to the countryside." Michallon took his students outdoors to work directly from nature; they studied landscapes in the Paris region—Neuilly, Saint-Cloud, the forest of Fontainebleau—and farther afield, in Normandy. "I made my first open-air landscape in Arcueil under the supervision of this painter [Michallon]," Corot said later, "whose only advice was to render most scrupulously everything I saw before me. The lesson was a good one; I have loved precision ever since."

In the late eighteenth century Pierre Henri de Valenciennes, an exceptional theorist, founded the movement that would later be known as Neoclassical landscape. Using Poussin as a model, Valenciennes felt that the ultimate aim of a landscape painter's work was the quest for ideal Beauty, a representation of nature as it should be; and the culminating works of an artist's career were the studio compositions of large landscapes filled with figures. Above, his *Cicero Discovering the Tomb of Archimedes.*

Neoclassicism

The artistic milieu in which Corot was immersed during his training played a pivotal role in all his work. Neoclassicism was the reigning style at the time. Pierre Henri de Valenciennes, its primary supporter, had developed a new theory of landscape painting: using imagination only, the true landscape painter invented credible natural worlds. Open-air studies, which formed the artist's visual repertory, were preliminary steps to the creative work in the studio, where the painter worked from memory. The most famous painters of this movement included Jean Joseph Xavier Bidauld (1758–1846), Jean-Victor Bertin (1767–1842), François-Marius Granet (1775–1849) and, of course, Achille Etna Michallon. For these champions of an idealized nature, the most noble genre was historical landscape, which involved illustrating a mythological, literary or religious story in a landscape. *Narcissus Admiring his Reflection in the Water,* (left), by Pierre Henri de Valenciennes, is a brilliant example of such work.

Northern realism

Another landscape movement developed between 1780 and 1820 in France, based on the realism of seventeenth-century Flemish and Dutch landscape painters. Some landscapists were drawn more to the simplicity of the Flemish plains and forests of Île-de-France than to the antique grandeur of Italy. During the Ancien Régime, Jean Louis Demarne (1744–1829), Lazare Bruandet (1755–1803), Louis-Gabriel Moreau (1740–1806) and Georges Michel (1763–1843; left, *Cut Tree Lying Across a Forest Road*) imitated the realistic techniques of the northern painters, particularly in the use of precise brushstrokes to render the relationship between the subject and the light. Freed from literary or historical subjects, their paintings were meant to be topographically exact depictions of existing sites.

Following the principles of Neoclassicism to the letter, Michallon also encouraged his students to work from memory. "We therefore also urge that when you have made a study, you do it again without looking at the model; and after working to remember every element, you then compare this with the original," wrote Valenciennes.

Unfortunately, the period Corot spent working with this sensitive and talented master, whom he seemed to appreciate as a friend, ended suddenly and tragically after only a few months when Michallon died of pneumonia on September 24, 1822.

From Michallon to Bertin

When discussing Corot's artistic education, his biographers all stress his training in open-air painting; yet by this time, Corot had already developed his own approach to landscapes: he was working to balance the realism of landscapes painted on site with the imaginative "memory" work done later in the studio.

After Michallon's death, Corot naturally turned to his first master's former professor, Jean-Victor Bertin,

During his trip to Italy, Michallon made realistic reproductions of nature (above, *Cascades of Tivoli*). He then used these views to create large compositions (left, *Theseus Pursuing the Centaurs,* painted in 1821).

a brilliant product of the Neoclassical style. History painting was David's realm, while Bertin was the master of landscape. With Bertin, Corot worked as before, alternating open-air studies with studio work: drawings of antique models and collections of engravings of plants and trees, as well as copies of old masters.

Corot reproached Bertin for not teaching him the basic techniques of drawing. Yet it was Bertin who instilled in Corot the essential characteristics of the landscape. "The two things that seem to me to be of primordial importance are the strict study of drawing and of values," he wrote in one of his notebooks around 1825, at the time full of admiration for his professor's instruction. These notebooks, which are both intimate diaries and class notes, demonstrate his loyalty to Neoclassical principles and the determination of his research. "Draw every evening; small contemporary figures;... different kinds of trees; a few compositions from my studies; give myself subjects with historical figures; make copies from the *Annales des Beaux-Arts.*" Corot made endless copies of paintings by the masters in the Louvre, landscapes by Gaspard Dughet, Van Blœmen and Claude Lorrain.

Corot was particularly critical of his second master's teaching methods, declaring to a former fellow student, "I wasted my time in father Bertin's studio; I cannot manage to produce the least drawing." Bertin, however, was not only the most famous landscape painter in Paris during the Restoration; he had also studied at the Académie Royale school, and then later with Pierre Henri de Valenciennes. In addition to Michallon, Bertin trained many students in the Neoclassical tradition, including Jules Coignet (1798–1860) and Léon Fleury (1804–1858), artists Corot met again during his trip to Rome in 1825. Bertin was a fervent practitioner of his own teaching: he constantly worked on open-air studies, such as the *View near Essonnes,* (above).

Corot and the outdoors

After painting two or three times in Paris—where he created the magnificent view of *The Old Saint-Michel Bridge in Paris*—Corot worked on his first open-air studies in Normandy in August of 1822. He rediscovered his childhood memories in Bois-Guillaume with his friends, the Sennegon family, who had become relatives when Annette Octavie married Laurent Denis Sennegon. He selected simple, non-picturesque subjects: a field near Bois-Guillaume or the gate to his friends' property.

He concentrated on studying light and volumes. He forged his style of interpreting objects and natural elements, using quick brushstrokes and many layers of paint. Using the same technique, he painted a small seascape in the summer of 1822 in the town of Dieppe, perhaps alongside Michallon himself, in which he tried to capture the reflections of light on the water and in the sky. He also continued his work on seascapes in other studies, such as *Honfleur: The Old Wharf.*

Corot's favorite region, however, and one he painted over and over again, was the intimate and poetic world of Ville-d'Avray (to the west of Paris between Saint-Cloud and Versailles), where his parents had purchased a summer house. "Providence made Ville-d'Avray for Corot, just as

Even in Corot's earliest paintings—open-air studies he never intended to exhibit—he did not seek out attractive subjects or original viewpoints. All he cared about were the rendering of the skies, the effects of light on the buildings and the use of the painting medium—glazes or layers of paint—to imitate nature.

"Imagine that two absolutely identical objects exist: the sun would not light them up in the same way."

Corot

Sky, architecture and water were three of the elements that fascinated the young artist during working trips to Honfleur (far left, *Honfleur: The Old Wharf*) or in Paris (left, *The Old Saint-Michel Bridge in Paris*). In both these works, Corot concentrated on two particular aspects of the landscape. First, he explored the role of light in the pictorial composition of the buildings of Notre-Dame and the tower of the Honfleur port; and secondly, he studied the way each element stood out against a light-colored sky. For his view of Paris, the Seine gave him the opportunity to study the reflections of water. And oddly enough for a seascape, the presence of water in the Honfleur painting is suggested only by the masts and sails of the boats.

Corot was made for Ville-d'Avray," wrote Étienne Moreau-Nélaton, stressing Corot's sentimental and lifetime attachment to this landscape of ponds and woods.

The ponds of Ville-d'Avray

Corot felt that these first open-air paintings, begun in 1822, were extremely important to his development. In them, he defined his own technique, adjusting his own personality to the teachings of his masters. "Sketch as closely as possible to the color and go over it with a glaze of clarified poppy-seed oil. Lay paint on over this glaze after drawing all the masses."

The Cabassud Houses at Ville-d'Avray, one of his first masterpieces, dates from this period. It depicts a small path running along the Corot property that leads to a group of houses known by the name of the owner, M. Cabassud. Corot often returned to the composition of this view; the aesthetic foundations for his entire career were formed around this family property. He also worked in the nearby woods above the ponds, painting *Ville-d'Avray: Edge of the Woods with a Woman Cowherd,* a pretty, realistic canvas later reworked with the painter Diaz de la Peña. Another of these works is the *Little Chaville,* in which the contrast between light and dark, and the rendering of the leaves are already well mastered, although the figures seem to be too small in relation to the landscape.

After finishing his classes in Bertin's studio and working in Ville-d'Avray and Normandy, Corot gathered up enough courage to attempt his first studio landscape, *Orpheus.* The figures in this mythological work are still stiff and the work strongly reflects the influences of Lorrain and especially Bertin and Michallon. But Corot's talent is already evident in the reflections of the pond in the foreground, the treatment of the trees and the charming landscape of mountains and seaside in the background. Once Corot

In Corot's first paintings, he seemed to be looking at familiar sites to find austere subjects that had no picturesque or romantic embellishments, so that he could fully concentrate on the technical aspects of his work. Île-de-France, particularly the region of Ville-d'Avray, offered calm,

simple scenes that he painted just as he saw them. In *Little Chaville* (above), a simple dirt path is the focal point, while in *The Cabassud Houses at Ville-d'Avray* (left), the lane at the edge of his parents' property seems to be the true center of the painting.

Corot's parents purchased the Ville-d'Avray house in March of 1817. Camille immediately claimed a room on the third floor at the west side of the house, with two windows facing the pond adjoining the property.

had acquired a solid technique in open-air landscape painting, he was able to move on to the next, indispensable stage in the training of early nineteenth-century painters: the time-honored trip to Italy.

Corot and Diaz both reworked certain sections of *Edge of the Woods with a Woman Cowherd* (above).

"I noticed that everything that was done correctly on the first attempt was more true, and the forms more beautiful.... I also see how important it is to be exacting when working from life, and not be satisfied with a hasty sketch. How many times in reviewing my drawings have I regretted not having had the courage to stay an extra half-hour!... One must not allow indecision in a single thing."

Corot

CHAPTER TWO
THE FIRST TRIP TO ROME (1825–1828)

In Italy, Corot alternated drawing and painting for the open-air studies he made throughout Rome (left, detail of *Rome: The Coliseum Seen Through Arches of the Basilica of Constantine*) and in the nearby countryside. He also patiently studied the figure (right, a page from one of his sketchbooks).

In 1825, probably on the advice of Jean-Victor Bertin, Corot decided to ask his parents to finance a trip to Italy for several years. The "large, timid and awkward child," who "blushed whenever anyone talked to him" and was embarrassed "in front of the beautiful ladies in his mother's shop," had finally grown into a painter confident in his craft and his vocation.

Pierre Henri de Valenciennes also made open-air studies of Roman sites, capturing the subtle, transparent effects of light on the buildings (left).

The call of ancient Rome

Corot's master Michallon was one of the landscape artists most inspired and impassioned by his travels in Italy. During the three years he lived in Rome, Michallon painted sublime, luminous open-air views, demonstrating his astonishing ability to create a pictorial transcription of space. Corot, who copied these paintings, often heard his master speak movingly of Roman monuments and Sicilian landscapes. Later, when he was studying with Bertin, Corot learned to place antique ruins in a historical landscape in the manner of Poussin. His desire to visit Italy naturally grew along with his increasing knowledge.

Since the seventeenth century the rite of the Italian tour had become an essential step for every young artist, especially one as conscientious as Corot, who wanted to follow in the footsteps of his illustrious predecessors.

This academic desire was mixed with other, more personal motivations. "In 1826," wrote Théophile Silvestre, "Corot went to live in Rome, not to receive an official education, but to enjoy the beautiful weather and work the whole year round in the open air, something that was impossible to do in the more variable climate of Paris." But he was mistaken about Corot's true intentions, which were to take the theories of his Neoclassical education and apply them in practice. Like many painters before him, Corot traveled first to Rome to discover antiquity and the grandeur of its architecture. Along with this quest for antique sources and a different cultural and geographical environment,

"Italy! Italy! This is the desire of all artists who start to feel the beauties of their art and who have the enthusiasm of talent," wrote Valenciennes in his landscape treaty (1800), the main reference for all young painters in Corot's time. Before starting their career, they were expected to tour the European country with the greatest number of antique sources. During this rite of initiation, they discovered the beautiful Mediterranean light and its sites, so well-suited to the study of landscape painting. Below, a view of Rome from the hills, ca. 1800.

Corot intended to work on open-air landscapes.

Traveling to Italy

Corot convinced his parents of the necessity of this trip. He left home for the first time in his adult life at the age of 29. His father completely financed the trip and his expenses in Italy, and even agreed to pay for an additional year, on a single, rather affectionate condition: Corot had to leave behind a self-portrait. Just before leaving, then, he painted one of the first portraits of his career, his own.

At the time there were two ways to travel overland to Italy: through the French Riviera and Genoa, or over the Alps via the Simplon pass and the Trento Valley. An alternative possibility was to take a boat from Marseilles directly to an Italian port, but Corot did not want to miss the alpine scenery. He decided to go through Switzerland and into Italy by way of the Alps. As he went through Lausanne, he painted a view of the city and of Lake Geneva. He wandered through Tuscany before going to Rome. A letter dated December 2, 1825, to his friend Abel Osmond, his confidant during the trip to Italy, reveals that his interest in some of these towns was not purely painterly.

The reversed image of the artist, viewed in a mirror, in his first self-portrait.

"Oh Abel, never go through Bologna. This town has too many seductive beauties. I smile. I let myself fall for the most seductive *balarina* in the Bologna Opera, delivered to us for our comfort, after a difficult and especially exciting trip."

In December of 1825, soon after arriving in Rome, Corot found a room on the fourth floor of the Palazzo dei Pupazzi on the via del Capo di Case. It was near the piazza di Spagna, the Trinità dei Monti and the Villa Medici, which housed the Academy of France and the Prix de Rome *pensionnaires.* He gave his parents and Parisian friends a mailing address at the famous Caffè Greco, the meeting place for all the young artists and intellectuals of Rome.

"Vedute di Roma"

"I cannot write about the climate in Rome; it has been raining as long as I've been here," he wrote to Abel Osmond. "But it doesn't bother me, I was forewarned." Later in the same letter, he complained of feeling far from home. Although the rain prevented Corot from working full time on his landscapes during the first few months, he used the rooftops of Rome as subjects, which he painted from the window of his room. He went to the Forum to study the ancient Roman

Corot still appears somewhat awkward in this first self-portrait. He wanted to depict himself seated at his easel, working at his craft. Curiously, despite his good-natured personality, in this work he painted himself in the shadows, in a rather romantic style; indeed, he seems to look worried. Yet this is the portrait of an amiable man, who held his friends spellbound with his enthusiasm during interminable conversations in Roman taverns. The artists set up their headquarters in the Caffè Greco, sharing their passions and convictions over glasses of Italian wine. At the end of one long day of work, after several people criticized the overly realistic aspect of Corot's paintings, another painter, Théodore Caruelle d'Aligny (1798–1871), scolded the group, "My friends, Corot is our master!"

monuments, particularly the Coliseum, which he rendered skillfully in a view through the arches of the Basilica of Constantine. This small study is a perfect example of the Neoclassical style, strongly influenced by David. The columns, which define the space, provide a setting for the real subject of the painting in the background: the Coliseum. Corot worked on the sites praised by Michallon—for example, *View of the Villa Medici*—and drew his inspiration from Bertin's studio paintings. Concerned purely with technical questions, he did not allow any emotional expression in his work, and worked to attain a synthesis of light and space.

Corot returned to the subjects favored by the eighteenth-century classical and *vedute* painters (who painted topographically correct "viewpoints" of famous places). He painted the banks of the Tiber River and the Castel Sant'Angelo. Following the example of Vanvitelli and Joseph Vernet, he set up outdoors in front of the San Spirito Hospital, not far from the via della Conciliazione—which placed the Castel Sant'Angelo in the center of his composition—or upstream from the Ponte Sant'Angelo, using the bridge, the castle and Saint Peter's dome to create a continuous painterly composition. These exceptional open-air views—which are intensely luminous and painted with strong brushstrokes—were then reworked in the

The Trinità dei Monti (left) is one of five French churches in Rome; it was constructed on orders of King Charles VIII of France in 1495. It was also one of Corot's favorite places to work: he painted no less than five canvases of this church overlooking the city of Rome.

L'Académie de France 1826-27.

Corot often painted near the Villa Medici, which housed the French Academy in Rome. He made panoramic views from a window or from the gardens, just as all the *pensionnaires* before him had done since the start of the century. He never won the Prix de Rome, but his presence alone in Italy is enough to prove his attachment to artistic tradition.

Corot en avait fait une ou deux ou trois copies.

studio; Corot painted several versions from these studies, to which he added figures.

He also painted vast overviews in which he used light to construct space. For subjects he chose a view of the Trinità dei Monti and a panorama of Rome from the Villa Medici, with the famous antique marble basin in the foreground.

Views of the Forum from the Farnese Gardens

In early 1826, despite his self-doubts and anxieties, Corot painted three masterpieces representing the

Coliseum and the Forum, viewed from the Farnese Gardens. At three different times of day—morning, noon and evening—he painted three different views from three different angles, still employing a classical style. Seventeenth-century artists often painted the gardens of the Villa Farnese, and Valenciennes had advised his students to follow Claude Lorrain's example and work from

“For one month now, I have been awakened every morning by bright sunlight that strikes the wall of my room.... But I find this brilliant sun dispiriting. I feel the complete impotence of my palette.”

Corot

the Palatine Hill. Corot's paintings of the Forum from this viewpoint were therefore not revolutionary. Indeed, he worked alongside several other artists, including Brascassat and Ernest Fries.

Corot's real innovation, however, was his decision to vary the viewpoints of these three studies depending on the time of day. They were each painted during long sessions outdoors and undoubtedly considerably reworked later in the studio. Corot selected these viewpoints with great care, and each of his studies was oriented along the path of the sun: in the morning he painted the San Sebastiano Church to the east; at noon the Coliseum toward the northeast; and in the evening he worked on the sunset over the Forum to the west.

The young painter conscientiously applied the principles he learned in Paris, while gradually adding a more personal note to his open-air studies. This was the first time Corot attempted this idea of working at different times of day; he used it again in several canvases he submitted to the Salons.

“Opposite him, the Coliseum emerges from the heart of the antique city, dominates the blue horizon of the mountains with its hot red mass. The light has just changed, another has replaced it, and without leaving the terrace of the Farnese Gardens, changing only his point of view, he obstinately continues his task.”

Moreau-Nélaton

The three views of the San Sebastiano Church (bottom left), the Coliseum (below) and the Forum (top left), made in 1826 from the Farnese gardens, were painted, respectively, in the morning, noon and evening.

Figure studies

As required by the trip to Italy, Corot also accepted the obligation to study the human figure.

Aside from the self-portrait he left with his family and a few rare figures painted in Dieppe and Fontainebleau, Corot had rarely portrayed the figure. Indeed, in Rome, he complained that he could not manage to capture in his drawings the movement of children at play. When the weather was bad, he chose models at random in the streets and tried to reproduce their poses and clothing. This study of local color was also a required exercise for painters who later would have to add figures to their studio landscape compositions. Corot accepted this obligation, and in so doing, discovered a new passion that soon became an essential element in his work: the human figure.

During this period he began to invent the genre of "imaginary figures" that he often painted in the second half of his career. He brought together his love of bright clothing, his interest in the pictorial interpretation of character and his capacity to capture and render the harmony of human expression.

In 1708, Roger de Piles, a major theorist of classical painting, stressed the relationship between the landscape and figures. "I am convinced that the best way to bring out figures is to match them so well to the character of the landscape that it seems as though the landscape itself was created for the figures."

Corot studied figures assiduously, drawing with pencil and pen-and-ink during walks through the streets of Rome and in the Italian countryside. These drawings were spontaneous and quickly executed works taken from life (left, woman with a tambourine).

A study of the *Ponte Nomentano* hanging behind the *Seated Italian Youth in Corot's Room* situates the site where the work was painted. The notes drawn up by Alfred Robaut (left, one of these notes), used for the *Catalogue raisonné* of Corot's work, indicate that at least three versions of this figure exist.

In the studio, Corot drew his figures with a stark honesty, sometimes even making his models look deliberately miserable (far left, *Two Italians*). Yet he also appreciated the nobility of an old man's head or the innocence of a child (below and left) in his search for models to use as religious figures or antique heroes.

He used all kinds of models, from an old man dressed up as a peasant or a monk to a young boy posing in a corner of his studio. He could also capture the sheen of colored cloth and render the sensuality of the beautiful Italian women.

The figure studies painted during this first trip to Italy are striking for their contrasting light, sober models and unadorned realism. The artist's greatness appears in these faces as much as in his landscapes.

The Roman countryside

In May of 1826, after temporarily exhausting the beauties of the capital, Corot started traveling through the

VENTE
COROT

“You ask me for news of the Roman women. They are still the most beautiful women in the world I've ever seen. I had some from time to time, but it costs me. They are not all voluptuous.... Despite that, their eyes, shoulders, hands and asses are superb.... As a painter, I prefer Italian women, but in terms of sentiment, I go more for the French.”
Letter to Abel Osmond

Corot's letters reflect his great passion for

the female body. Like his master Michallon (above) or other painters from this period, such as Léon Cogniet (left), Corot used his time far from the constraints of Parisian conventions to study the female figure and to work on the beautiful effects of the colorful regional costumes (far left, *Young Italian Woman from Papigno with Her Distaff*).

Italian countryside to satisfy another obligation of Neoclassical training: the quest for contrasting pastoral landscapes. He left Rome and went north along the Tiber toward the landscapes where Poussin himself is supposed to have worked (*The Poussin Promenade*). Corot then traveled to the region of the Sabine mountains, first stopping in the village of Civita Castellana, nestled in the midst of wild, rocky gorges and sheer mountains. The landscapes he painted in this region are particularly interesting: they reveal the training of a young artist working hard to perfectly master the various methods of painting trees and rocks.

Corot found this region exceptionally inspiring. He worked with oil and pencil alongside Édouard Bertin and Ernest Fries, producing about thirty oil paintings during this time. He discovered such a wealth of subjects in Civita Castellana that he returned in 1827.

Corot continued to Papigno, a small mountain village near Terni, where he spent the entire summer of 1826. It was during this trip to Papigno, which he used as a base to paint the Cascade of Terni and Lake Piediluco, that he wrote to Abel Osmond, admitting

Corot was enchanted by the variety of the sites in the mountainous regions of the Italian countryside, which alternated between forests, plains, streams, lakes, mountains and valleys, (bottom right, a drawing made in Civita Castellana; top right, *Papigno: Buildings Overlooking the Valley*; above, *The Poussin Promenade*). He studied trees and rocks —"nature's main ornaments,"—which were the basics of classical landscapes. He heeded Pierre de Valenciennes' advice and kept the various studies, drawn or painted on paper, "in a portfolio to be consulted and used again, when needed."

his desire to work exclusively on his painting. "I have only one aim in life, which I want to pursue steadfastly; to make landscapes. This firm resolution will not allow any serious attachments. By this I mean marriage." From Papigno, Corot traveled to

While Corot's drawings were highly spontaneous, his painted studies from 1826 onward became increasingly constructed. He structured his landscapes, defining the various planes and lines of sight that create the perspective. The view of the village of Papigno (above) is remarkable in this respect: a powerful diagonal movement divides the work in half, while the succession of fields reaching to the mountains in the background creates the sense of depth. Corot used a system of visual references to help him when he returned to paint in the studio.

The foreground in this open-air study, *Ponte Narni* (left), has all the characteristics of a work painted from life. Corot concentrated on treating the light that strikes the bridge pilings, and bathes the river and plants in sunlight (below, detail).

Narni, several miles away, to the hilltops overlooking the Nera River, a tributary of the Tiber.

Ponte Narni

Like Michallon and Bertin before him, Corot painted the antique ruins of the bridge at Narni, which was constructed over the Nera during the reign of Emperor Augustus. This open-air oil study, a marvel of transparency and contrast, is considered by art historians to be one of Corot's major works from Italy, due to the mixture of pictorial innovation and Neoclassical influences, even in the handling of the mountains in the background. Yet Corot was merely employing the open-air techniques that all painters were supposed to use.

The following winter, he returned to this subject to create a studio composition that he submitted to the 1827 Salon. Thanks to a preparatory drawing, we know that Corot had decided to move the point of view in the finished painting farther away from the bridge, and that he had already planned to position a group of trees on the left and two umbrella pines in the center of the painting. Indeed, the drawing differs from the final painting in one aspect only: four cows, which in the drawing were fording the Nera, in the company of a cowherd, disappeared in the painting, replaced by several goats moving down a path on the left side of the canvas.

Even in this study, *Ponte Narni* demonstrates Corot's instinctive brilliance in depicting the effects of light. The work, recreated in the studio with a dramatic content and format that were more acceptable to the Salon, retains some of these aspects, particularly on the path and the figures.

The painting was exhibited at the Salon of 1827, along with another work, *La Cervara,* a rugged description of an approaching storm just before twilight. A fervent champion of classical themes, Corot considered these two works to be complementary, one depicting the morning, the other the evening. The Salon critics received Corot's first submitted paintings with neither enthusiasm nor

In *La Cervara* (above), Corot created a marvelous synthesis of elements from classical landscape masters: Poussin, for the buildings ornamenting the mountains in the background; and Claude Lorrain, for the effects of light and his experience in the realistic representation of nature, acquired during his Italian trip. The contrast between the shadow and the light, the almost romantic dramatization and the realism of the landscape are undeniable qualities of this masterpiece.

The study for *Ponte Narni* (far left) was made in the morning: the horizontal sunlight streams in from the right-hand side of the work, from Narni located to the east.

hostility, although the paintings revealed a mature artist, who was a direct descendant of Valenciennes and Michallon, skilled in the Neoclassical theories very much in fashion at the time.

Benefits of the first Italian trip

By the end of 1826 Corot had had enough of antique monuments, and made short trips to Albano, Nemi, Rocca di Papa, Ariccia, Frascati and Marino, ending his travels in Tivoli in December. In 1827 he worked in Olevano in April, Marino in May, and then during the summer, again painted Lake Albano, Civitella and Subiaco. He developed his technique and perfected his realist and precise observation of nature.

Throughout the entire year of 1827, despite clear progress, he still seemed to doubt his abilities and

produced fewer works than he had the previous summer in Civita Castellana and Narni. "Today, we flatter ourselves, we consider ourselves to be superior geniuses," he wrote to his friend Osmond. "Tomorrow, we will be ashamed of our works, we can't do anything.... I have just returned from the countryside: well, I'm not very pleased with myself. Let's hope that I'll have a better day tomorrow."

In Rome Corot discovered the multiple facets of his craft. He began to understand his own unique qualities and also learned to work alongside other artists, to share a motif with fellow painters. Indeed, far from being a solitary artist, an innovative genius, as some art historians have portrayed him, during his Italian trip Corot was a young painter who skillfully applied the Neoclassical principles and was happily consumed with the Mediterranean light, a passion that remained with him throughout his life.

Corot met many painters who were also staying in the Italian capital. He was friendly with the landscapists Auguste Lapito (1803–1874), Guillaume Bodinier (1795–1872) and Léopold Robert (1794–1835), who

all suggested he should study Italian costumes. He deepened his friendship with two painters he had met in Michallon's studio, and met two other men who became his close friends: Édouard Bertin (1797–1871) and Théodore Caruelle d'Aligny (1798–1871).

This *View from Narni*, submitted to the Salon of 1827, was often compared to the study of the *Ponte Narni*. Yet it was discredited; because it was less spontaneous than the study, it contained less of Corot's creative genius. However, this viewpoint ignores the Neoclassical tenet that distinguished between a study and the same subject recreated in the studio, a work intended for the Salon.

One of the essential benefits of the Italian trip to Corot's career was his acceptance in the professional artistic milieu and the creation of a network of lifelong friendships. These artists made many quick sketches of each other at work (top, Mount Vesusius, in Corot's sketchbook; below, Corot seated in the grass, by A. Colin).

Just as Michallon eight years earlier, Corot spent the entire summer of 1828 on the coast around Naples. He painted landscapes around Vesuvius and produced deceptively simple, luminous and beautiful views in Naples, Amalfi and Capri. At the end of the summer, Corot finally returned to France, stopping in Venice and Genoa for a final look at the Italian landscape.

After learning the theories of landscape painting in the studios of Michallon and Bertin, then working on his own in the countryside around Rome, Corot began to create idealized landscapes in 1830. Yet he continued to refine his subject matter, "to practice his scales," in the French countryside. Remaining aloof from the aesthetic debates raging around him, Corot submitted entries to the Salons that reflected his desire to alternate between mythological and religious themes.

CHAPTER THREE

THE BEGINNING OF A CAREER (1828–1844)

More professional than ever in this second self-portrait, Corot confidently played with the artifices of the mirror by holding the brush and palette in his left hand. On his return from Italy, he decided to use the many drawings made during his travels for the large compositions sent to the Salon.

By this time, Corot had finally won his artistic independence. He furthered his Neoclassical training by studying the northern landscapists, the Flemish and Dutch artists. He also liked contemporary English painters, particularly their realistically painted forest views and luminous, panoramic landscapes. The influence of Ruisdael and Berchem—whose works have been in the Louvre since the eighteenth century—is clear in such works as *View in the Forest of Fontainebleau,* which he exhibited in the Salon of 1831. During the 1830s, Corot was fascinated by the work of John Constable (1776–1837); he was able to study the Englishman's canvases in an odd little brasserie on the rue Saint-Martin, where the dealer Thomas Arrowsmith exhibited English paintings.

Fontainebleau, an extension of Italy

Valenciennes encouraged the regular discipline of open-air painting, even after his students had completed their training. The Neoclassical artists had discovered a vast source of inspiration in the forests of Île-de-France, some twenty years before the Romantic painters. When the landscape artist could not travel to Italy—such as when Corot decided to postpone a trip to Rome in 1835 after the outbreak

Narcisse Diaz de la Peña, a Spanish artist whose love of painting brought him to France, often worked at Fontainebleau in the mid-1830s. More romantic and passionate than Corot, he preferred turbulent sites (left), such as the place called "Jean de Paris" in the heart of the forest.

With Théodore Rousseau (below), Corot shared a discreet, loyal and respectful friendship. Rousseau liked only Corot's open-air work, finding his other paintings too classical and serene. Corot, however, remained stongly influenced by Rousseau's vision, which encompassed lyrical, romantic, expressive and even brutal themes, such as *Road in the Forest of Fontainebleau, Effect of a Storm,* (left). But Théodore Rousseau had completely abandoned studio painting, while Corot, who used open-air work to expand his experience, generally created his masterpieces in the calm of his studio.

of a cholera epidemic—subjects well suited to open-air painting were readily available in the countryside around Fontainebleau. The diverse subject matter, the balanced light, and the pure, untouched nature in this Île-de-France region gave him a substitute for Italy.

The Forest Services maintained a strict control over the use of this land. It was forbidden, for example, to graze cattle, cut wood or light fires within the forest. This created an ideal situation for painters, who could find the desolate sites they needed for history painting. Corot was preparing his first large biblical landscapes for the Salon and found the austere elements he needed in this wild, untamed nature.

In Fontainebleau, Corot made realistic and strong landscapes, painted with thick, energetic and rough brushstrokes, working to create layers of paint and depict the effects of light. He represented nature for nature's sake, motivated by pure pleasure, although he often reused these studies later for large historical compositions: a study of a grove of oak trees was placed in *Hagar in the Wilderness,* a work exhibited in the 1835 Salon; and the enormous tree in *"The Raging One"* was placed in the composition of *Flight into Egypt,* painted in 1840 for the church at Rosny-sur-Seine. Yet *"The Raging One"* and *The Apremont*

Corot drew his inspiration from the most picturesque, well-known sites in Fontainebleau, views that painters felt obliged to paint. He used *"The Raging One"* (above) as a subject several times; indeed, the bare silhouette reappeared in several of his historical landscapes.

Gorges at Fontainebleau were fully realized works in themselves, even if Corot did not exhibit them. He reused the sites of Fontainebleau in several paintings submitted to the Salons of 1831 and 1833, but these works were always completely recomposed in the studio, with the additional inspiration of Ruisdael and Constable.

The famous boulders in the Fontainebleau forest were studied by many painters. Combined with *"The Raging One"* (left, represented in an engraving of the time), they create the backdrop for the painting above. As opposed to Corot's Italian views, which rarely contained people, the originality of his Fontainebleau works lay in his attempts to place figures within the landscapes. His motivation was clear: to learn to introduce figures and animate the body within a natural environment, in order to paint credible historical landscapes.

The figure in the landscape

Although Corot worked constantly at Chailly and Barbizon, where he went almost every year, he remained untouched by the debate surrounding the Romantic school. Moreau-Nélaton was surprised by his extreme reserve in response to a revolt in 1835 by the younger generation against what they considered to be a gross injustice, the repeated refusal of the Salon jury to show works by Théodore Rousseau:

Corot often visited Rouen, where he stayed with the Sennegon family in Bois-Guillaume, as in his youth. He had made enormous progress since his first studies in 1822 and when he painted the town from the Saint-Catherine hillside (left), he included the meanders of the Seine, the cathedral towers and the nearby hills into a superb panorama, as if he were viewing them from the heights of the Palatine Hill in Rome. He reworked this study the following year in a large composition for the Salon; however, that work was never exhibited there.

"During the battle that pits the innovators against the traditionalists, Corot keeps one foot planted in each camp, or rather, he remains distant from both." The ambitions of Théodore Rousseau, whose landscapes contained no figures at all and were intended to express the inner state of the painter, could not have been more different from Corot's outlook, which is probably the reason for his cool reaction.

The figures that always appear in his landscapes—a young shepherdess, a goatherd, a simple passerby—such as in *Quarry of the Chaise-Marie at Fontainebleau* or *Rocks at Fontainebleau,* reflect the humanist intentions of his Neoclassical view of nature. From the deepest thickets, a small peasant girl always gazes out at the viewer.

The light of Normandy

In the forests of Île-de-France, Corot concentrated primarily on rocks and trees. In Normandy, however, he discovered an ideal spot

to study water and sky. He traveled frequently to Normandy, probably as often as he went to Chailly and Barbizon. He worked inland, near Rouen, and at the seaside in Le Havre, Honfleur and Trouville, developing technical innovations in his analysis of the complex interplay between light and space.

It was probably during a visit to the Saint-Siméon farm, perhaps in 1830, that he painted the study *Honfleur: Calvary on the Côte de Grâce,* which is a miraculous rendering of light. The spontaneity, realism and perfect depiction of light in his many seascapes all prefigure Eugène Boudin, Johann Barthold Jongkind and even Monet's early works in the 1860s. *Beached Ship at Trouville, Le Havre, The Sea Seen from the Cliffs* and *Fishermen's Houses at Sainte-Adresse* are all examples of Corot's use of rapid brushstrokes to capture the transparent quality of the air and the shimmering light. As opposed to the landscapes painted in the Fontainebleau forest, these Normandy scenes were only indirectly used in Corot's historical compositions. Furthermore, he never exhibited the open-air seascapes, with the exception of the 1834 Salon, in which he showed a view of the port of Rouen recreated in his studio. These Normandy studies were apparently painted purely for pleasure and to enrich his visual repertory.

In Normandy, where he stayed every year, Corot seems to have anticipated the work of the Impressionists: the clarity of his colors, the visible and lively brushstrokes, and the contrasting effects of light and dark are particularly well illustrated in this view of the bay at Le Havre, painted from the cliffs along the Côte de Grâce, north of Honfleur (above).

Around 1825, the famous Mère Toutain and her daughter opened the Saint-Siméon farm to travelers. Located in the hills above Honfleur, this inn was extremely popular among painters, who had only to walk a few yards for a view of the sea. Left, the farm painted by Corot and a photograph taken twenty years later, in the time of the Impressionists.

All this experience acquired during long and productive working sessions on site—the skillful mastery of light, space and volume, along with a realistic representation of the sites—came together in his first masterpiece, *Chartres Cathedral.*

A passion for architectural viewpoints

In 1830, Corot became worried during the July Revolution and left

Paris with a friend he met in Italy, the architect Poirot. The two men stopped at Chartres to paint the Gothic cathedral. Corot first worked on a view of the west door, trying to accurately and graphically render every possible detail of the architecture and the monumental sculpture. He then made an overall view of the cathedral, from the base of the old medieval village. He probably painted from life or at least partially so; it appears that he found shelter in a nearby house. Despite the obvious attraction to Gothic architecture, which is similar to the view of the Romantics, this exceptionally clear and simply defined work is still very much a product of his Neoclassical culture, particularly in the balanced

The imposing mound of earth in the foreground blocking the Gothic towers is proof that Corot conceived the *Chartres Cathedral* as an exercise, not as a finished painting.

composition and mastery of the effects of light on the volumes.

In the 1830s, Corot often created architectural studies of this kind to further the aesthetic theories first developed as he worked in front of the Castel Sant'Angelo or the Trinità dei Monti Church. Indeed, he sometimes combined these studies with large, panoramic views, such as *View of Saint-Lô* and *View of the Chateau of Pierrefonds.* He created landscapes that contained a direct and realistic beauty, which some people considered to be naive. Several other works can be included in this genre: *Orléans: View from a Window Overlooking the Saint-Paterne Tower* and the two works painted in 1833 for a friend, the textile industrialist Philibert-Paulin Henry, which are astonishing for their lucidity and sense of light and depth (*Soissons: House and Factory of Mr. Henry* and *Soissons Seen from Mr. Henry's Factory*). In these two paintings, along with *Chartres Cathedral,* Corot reached the summit of his technical skill in realistic landscape painting.
He had acquired the two principal qualities of the landscapist: sincerity and simplicity. Yet he retained the initial ideas of his classical education: to bare the internal structures of a site in order to recreate them in his painting.

A sketch of Chartres Cathedral (above) demonstrates that before painting on canvas, Corot worked out elements of the architecture in drawings. In 1872, he retouched the painting, deploring the fact that it was a "portrait of the towers without the atmosphere of Chartres." He then added a figure and extensively reworked the foreground.

From his meticulous studies of Roman monuments, Corot learned the importance of absorbing "the atmosphere of the site," as well as the precise rendering of the effect of light on stones, and the imitation of materials using a few layers of colors. He already had a sense of poetic ambiance, visible in the paintings of Chartres Cathedral (center) and the modest factory that belonged to one of his father's friends in Soissons (far left).

The poet of French landscape

Between 1830 and 1845, Corot traveled throughout France and made several other important trips to Switzerland to visit his friend Armand Leleux in Dardagny, and Baud-Bovy in the chateau of Gruyères. He worked in Auvergne, Provence, the Limousin, Burgundy and Isère, and traveled often to Brittany, the Morvan and the coast along the North Sea.

Sometimes, family attachments brought him to a region. This explains his paintings from the Morvan, where he visited his niece, Marie-Louise Laure Sennegon and her husband, Philibert Baudot. After the rich cultural sites of Italy, Corot developed new pictorial theories in Normandy and the Fontainebleau forest, while the Morvan gave Corot the opportunity to create realistic paintings of nature, with no poetic embellishment. Oddly enough, he rediscovered the noble composition and refined lighting of his

In Switzerland and in the Morvan, Corot alternated realistic drawings of peasant life (left, a washerwoman) with more tranquil paintings. The view of Mornex (top left) demonstrates his contribution to the pastoral landscape genre and reflects Corot's technical and plastic concerns: a maximum use of light, inventive composition and a precise description of the various pictorial planes as in *Saint-André-en-Morvan* (above) and *A Farm at Recouvrières, in the Nièvre* (following page).

Italian views when he painted a view of Lormes from his windows, as he had done in Rome in 1825. He captured the small village church with the same intensity as the Castel Sant'Angelo. In the same vein, the two unadorned views of Saint-André-en-Morvan attain a sublime beauty.

In Brittany, where he often stayed for long periods with other painters and people he knew from his cloth apprenticeship days, Corot worked to bring out the results of his research. In keeping with his Neoclassical ideal, he forced his hand to become an absolute extension of his eye. He constantly returned to the same elements —trees, skies, rivers, streams, homes of peasants and fishermen—and he never idealized nature, even preferring to hide regional architecture he felt was too picturesque under a silver-gray sky, such as in *Breton Women at the Fountain* Corot traveled from Brittany to the Charente region; the views of the *Port of La Rochelle* share the same quality of light as his Normandy seascapes.

Corot's landscapes painted at Saint-André-en-Morvan (above) were the antithesis of the Italian views: they contained no literary references, majestic natural sites or culture. Continuing his strictly technical studies, he described the changing perspective and colors resulting from the division of fields in space. As the poet of French landscape, he was depicting people of his own time, no longer nymphs and antique shepherds. This view (1842) anticipates the work of Jean-François Millet, who represented the poetic relationship between the peasant and nature.

Abel Osmond (left) met Corot in secondary school and by 1821 he had become the artist's close friend. This may have coincided with Corot's falling in love—reality or legend?—with Abel's aunt, Parfaite Anastasie Osmond. In any case, it was to Abel that Corot sent his most intimate impressions of his travels during his first trip to Italy. And it was Abel who posed in 1829 when Corot decided to try portraiture: he depicted his friend as slightly proud and determined. With his crossed arms, the young man seems to be measuring the viewer, as if to reflect his recent social success: he then had an important job in the Interior Ministry, after having worked as the minister's private secretary. The friendship between Corot and the Osmond family was profound and long-lasting, and Corot grieved deeply after Abel's early death in 1840.

Portraits and friends

After Corot returned from Italy, he alternated between painting landscapes and portraits, which several friends were urgently requesting. In 1829, he asked his mother's chambermaid Fanchette to pose, then portrayed three close friends, Abel Osmond, Alexandre Clérambault, nephew of his first employer M. Ratier, and Captain Faulte du Puyparlier.

A sensitive man, especially in the small circle of family and friends, Corot instilled in his portraits a warm and simple atmosphere, although his quest for realism remained as strong as ever. "You made him so ugly!" exclaimed his sister as she viewed the portrait of her son, Henri Sennegon. "I painted him as he is," was the painter's reply.

These first portraits still seem somewhat stiff and awkward, but the determinedly classical aspect

Corot's painting style was similar to that of Neoclassical portraits, as illustrated by Edmé Bochet (right), painted in 1811 by Ingres in Rome.

of these works, even in commissions for his friends, counterbalances these imperfections. From the Renaissance portraitists, he learned the technique of placing a somberly dressed model in front of an equally dark, uniform background. The subtle play of matching colors gave the painter the chance to display all his skill; indeed, only the face of the model catches the light and stands out from the shadows. Corot also used portraits by Ingres, which are beautifully realistic and graphically precise, as models for his research during this period.

Was it a family tradition (unconfirmed by any documents) that compelled Corot to paint a portrait of each of his nieces the year they turned sixteen? The portrait of the eldest, Marie-Louise Laure, was painted first, in 1831, followed by her sister Porphyre Marie-Denise Blanche; in 1833, he made another portrait of the third sister, Marie-Dorothée Joséphine, who was known as Octavie. Corot generally painted two copies, one for the model, the other for her mother. He used an identical method for each of these three portraits: the girl posed

Although he preferred women as models for his figures and portraits, Corot nevertheless painted several portraits of men, all characterized by stark realism, simple poses and invariably dark colors. Toussaint Lemaistre (above), engineer, architect and husband of one of Corot's nieces, Blanche Sennegon, is depicted in a strange manner: slouching slightly, with a hesitating expression and a hand placed soberly on his thigh. The armchair plays an important role in the pyramidal composition of this portrait.

standing up, "leaning on a small sewing table." The background, which remains in the shadows, was the interior of the family home. The format was the same for all three, at least before the portrait of Marie-Louise Laure was cut down on all four sides. Corot was able to combine a stark Neoclassicism with Romantic influences in these portraits of his

The graceful gesture of Louise Claire Sennegon's left hand, which seems to caress her cheek (above), softens this somewhat stiffly composed portrait.

nieces—particularly in the handling of the light and the choice of clothing. In 1837, he painted his sister's youngest daughter, Louise Claire. This time he drew his inspiration from English portraiture and altered the composition by placing the young girl in a landscape.

As usual, Corot made two copies of this portrait of Marie-Louise Laure Sennegon, another of his nieces: one was for the model, the other for her mother, Corot's older sister. Thanks to a drawing by Alfred Robaut — dutifully classified in the boxes now at the Louvre Museum (above) — we are certain that one version was cut down. The lower body of the girl, who was leaning on a sewing table, has disappeared. The other version, however, was not cut down, but was totally repainted by Corot after the early death of his niece.

Open-air synthesis

These beautiful family portraits—marked by a calm realism and spare composition—are superior examples of this nineteenth-century genre. Corot, however, soon became interested in a more poetic and freer interpretation of the human figure.

He had already made a portrait with the figure posed in a landscape, *Louise Harduin in Mourning,* painted in 1831. He repeated this in 1840 with the portrait of a young woman he may have been in love with, *Alexina Legoux,* who worked for his mother. Along with the portraits of Louise Claire Sennegon and François Auguste Biard, these rare examples of portraits painted outdoors reflect an attempt to synthesize his passion for nature and his portraiture technique. This concept was never really developed, as Corot made no more than about fifty portraits during his entire career.

He was perfecting his technique, and by 1840 he painted members of an even more intimate group: his sister Annette Octavie Sennegon, his brother-in-law Laurent Denis Sennegon and, around 1845, his mother. Finally, in a friendly gesture, he made

Louise Harduin (top left) and *The Blond Gascon* (above): from a personalized, "posed" portrait to an idealized depiction of the eternal feminine.

portraits of family members of the various friends who housed him during his travels throughout France and Switzerland. These included the Robert family, from Mantes, and the Delalain family. Édouard Delalain, the son of his former boss in the cloth trade, remained one of his closest friends throughout his life.

Starting in 1835, he began to further define his ideas and gradually freed himself from the traditional rules of portraiture to concentrate on a more depersonalized, fantastical interpretation of the figure. His first "imaginary figures," *Woman with a Sickle* and *The Blond Gascon* represent his idealization of models studied in the studio, as exemplars of eternal expressions or attitudes. Corot worked at the juncture of historical landscape painting, religious subjects and imaginary figures, sometimes draping an antique-style robe over his model, as in *Rébecca* or *Woman Reading with a Wreath of Flowers.*

Until 1860, Corot's figure studies and his historical landscape paintings were closely linked. *Woman Reading with a Wreath of Flowers* (above) is clearly part of the classical tradition: the figure in ancient clothes, reading soberly in an idealized landscape. At that time, Corot seemed to be trying to unite his two passions —women and landscape—in a single creation. Over time, the two genres gradually became independent again, and figure studies became an increasingly important part of his studio work.

A return to Italy

The ambitious landscapes—composed from studies made in Italy and in the forest of Fontainebleau—exhibited by Corot in the Salons of 1827, 1831, 1833 and 1834 encountered neither serious criticism nor decisive support. After wandering all over France, he felt a powerful desire to return to Italy. His decision can probably be

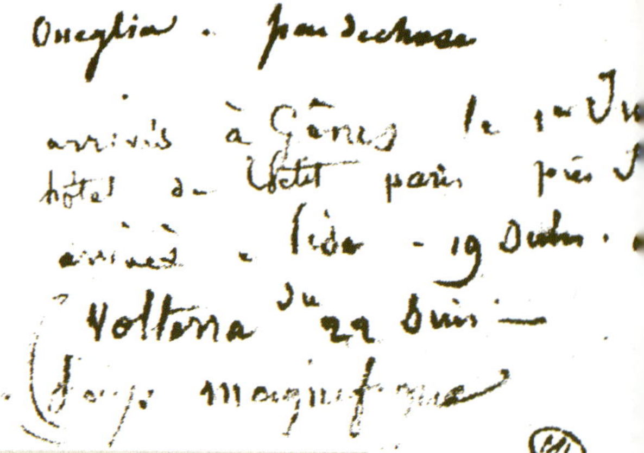

explained, at least in part, by his ambition to make a strong statement in the Salon with a large historical landscape. Indeed, he exhibited his first classical landscape composition, *Hagar in the Wilderness*, in

In 1833, Corot met the painter Grandjean, who accompanied him on his second trip to Italy in 1834. He immortalized his friend (left) at one of his favorite distractions: good food. The two men shared a keen sense of humor and a fondness for fine cuisine and wine, but Corot complained about his companion's indolence and lack of discipline for work. Indeed, his travel journal (top) makes no specific mention of Grandjean.

1835. In Italy, he was looking for inspiration for this important undertaking by drawing on the landscapes that had already stimulated his creativity.

Once again his father financed the trip, but did not want him gone for longer than six months. "We are no longer young, your mother and I; don't abandon us for a long time." Corot left for Italy in May of 1834 in the company of another painter, his friend Grandjean, whom he met in 1833 in Soissons. He kept detailed comments about all the practical details and anecdotes of his travels in a small notebook, interspersed with a few drawings sketched along the way.

Corot's travel notes contain a wealth of information: quick sketches of the various countrysides, notes about other travelers in the carriage and comments about the inns.

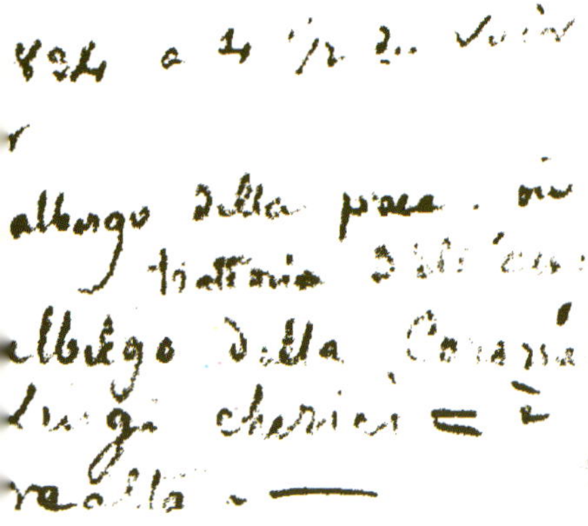

His itinerary was different from his first trip: crossing the Rhone Valley, stopping in Avignon and Marseilles, he arrived in Italy by way of Genoa, where he stayed two weeks and made three oil studies. The most captivating of these is clearly *Genoa Seen from the Acquasola Promenade* painted from the walkway running along the hills above the town, near the law

During Corot's second trip to Italy, the artist concentrated on his primary interests. He had already acquired the essential techniques of his craft by this time and he used drawing to take rapid notes: a few architectural elements or a ship that caught his eye (top right). He used oils for his carefully executed landscapes, as when he painted this wonderful view of Genoa from the gardens above the city. Indeed, the real subject of this landscape is the contrast between the foreground—overgrown and undefined, as usual—and the light-colored background depicting a group of houses.

courts and the San Stefano Church. This study reflects the artist's remarkable understanding of light and perspective: the sense of depth is accentuated by the almost monochromatic, light background behind an undefined foreground. Corot had indeed made considerable progress since his first trip to Italy!

From Volterra to Venice

After a short stop in Pisa, the painters continued on to Volterra, a "magnificent country" where they remained several weeks. In the area around this ancient city, Corot finally found the austere and luminous nature that would inspire his future compositions. He painted several open-air studies as well as two large canvases: *Volterra: The Citadel* and *Volterra: The Village.* These works provide tangible proof of a new maturity in the shimmering light, the effects of the visible, palpable brushstrokes, and the skillful understanding of the panoramic view.

Corot spent only a few days in Florence in July, where he made copies of Renaissance frescoes and painted two or three views of the city from the Boboli Gardens above the Palazzo Pitti. He finally arrived

Corot painted two opposing views of Volterra, situated on a high hill: the citadel (top right) and the village (bottom right). Several days later in Milan, he sketched two women, viewed from the back.

in Venice—which he had visited briefly in 1828 —and stayed for three full weeks. While studying Italian Renaissance paintings in the churches and palaces—his work would remain strongly influenced by Titian, Giorgione and Tintoretto—Corot painted views of the Grand Canal and the Piazzetta.
On his return, several collectors were entranced by the quality of the light in these works, as well as by the picturesque inetrpretation of this "gateway to the Orient," and Corot made several copies of these successful canvases.

The perfection of light

This second trip to Italy was productive. Corot achieved a perfection in his handling of light that he never again attained in the rest of his career. The open-air paintings gradually increased in precision, while they moved away from their initial purpose: no longer simple documents collected for later use in the studio, they took on the quality of finished works, both in technique and design.

On his first trip to Italy, when Corot passed through Venice, he felt that this historic city could be a rich source of inspiration. This time he spent long hours working at the historical sites, particularly the Piazzetta and the view toward Santa Maria della Salute, and San Giorgio Maggiore. Sometime around 1840, Corot used these studies again in commissions painted for several collectors; these later works have a more "touristy" aspect, although they retain the beautiful light of the Adriatic.

He used paper (glued to a stronger support for protection) less often than canvas, a revealing sign of his desire to show his productions, in one way or another, to the public and to his fellow painters.

His wanderings ended with a one-month stay in the lake region. Two studies—both extremely detailed—were made at Lake Garda, one at Dezenzano and the other at Riva. Corot then painted a single, remarkable work, *Lake Como and the Town.*

On his way back to France in the autumn of 1834, Corot was able to spend several days with his many Swiss friends and painted around Lake Geneva, in memory of the reveries of "the brilliant landscapist," Jean-Jacques Rousseau.

Using the small open-air study painted on paper at Riva (top left), Corot created a large painting (above), more acceptable to the Salon, where it was exhibited in 1835.

"Here, this is the tomb of Semiramis!": the historical landscape

Corot's direct communion with nature was so productive in France, Switzerland and Italy that it is possible to overlook the real purpose of his constant travels, which Corot considered to be an intermediate step in the creative process. During his walks, he often considered certain sites as future backdrops for his "subject" paintings. "Here, this is the tomb of Semiramis!" he cried when he saw a windmill near Arras. "This is the birthplace of Pericles!"

An open-air study made in the summer light was a pure pleasure, but it was ultimately intended for the hours spent reworking the canvas throughout the winter in the studio. "After my excursions," he said, "I invite Nature to spend a few days with me; this is when I start my folly: brush in hand, I look for hazelnuts in the woods in my studio; I hear the birds sing, the trees quiver in the wind, I see the rivers and streams run by, loaded with a thousand reflections of the sky and earth." Corot was still working at 15, quai Voltaire, in the studio near his mother's store, which he had rented in the early years of his training.

For Corot, it was inconceivable to exhibit a landscape painted solely from nature; studio work was therefore more important, as it was the only work seen by the public. To reach the summit of his craft, he still had to execute ambitious historical landscapes, which contained a mythological, literary or religious story. This was his goal for the Salon of 1835.

During Corot's second trip to Italy, he seemed to be painting happily without the technical anxieties of his first trip. He made lovely studies of regional costumes (above). At Lake Como, he recreated the spontaneous draftsmanship of works by Valenciennes and Michallon, combined with his own vivid technique.

Corot selected the same view as Valenciennes in 1780 for Lake Como (left): the leaves and bushes in the foreground, the lake in the center, and the mountains and sky occupying the upper half of the work. He used this composition repeatdly in his many paintings of the ponds at Ville-d'Avray.

"Hagar in the Wilderness"

Genesis, chapter 21, tells the story of Abraham's wife, Sarah, who—too old to have a child—advised her husband to conceive an heir with a young Egyptian slave named Hagar. She soon gave birth to a son, Ishmael. Through divine intervention, the aged Sarah became pregnant and also gave birth to a son, Isaac. One day, after Ishmael mocked Isaac, Sarah convinced Abraham to banish Hagar and her son, who wandered off into the desert and would have died without the intervention of an angel.

Corot may have used this rarely illustrated biblical theme in a preliminary sketch for a large painting in the winter of 1833–34, yet the project was soon abandoned.

This may explain Corot's trip to Italy in the summer of 1834. The desolate sites of Volterra were perfect for the theme of *Hagar in the Wilderness* and Corot, once again inspired by this subject, began work in the winter of 1834–35. He used a model for several drawing sessions to capture the dramatic pose of the main figure, the despairing Hagar, just as the angel appears in the distance. The passionate story and realistic handling of the extremely luminous background make this work a milestone in Corot's career.

Indeed, the artist was trying to revive the conventional genre of historical landscape through his love of nature. Alexandre Decamps, a Romantic painter who later became one of Corot's friends, wrote enthusiastically about this work in the *Revue républicaine.* "The feeling of an arid and forsaken nature, and the expanse of desert are understood unusually well; these contribute to the expression of distress the artist wanted to depict in the unfortunate Hagar, who implores the heavens as her last hope in the face of her despair."

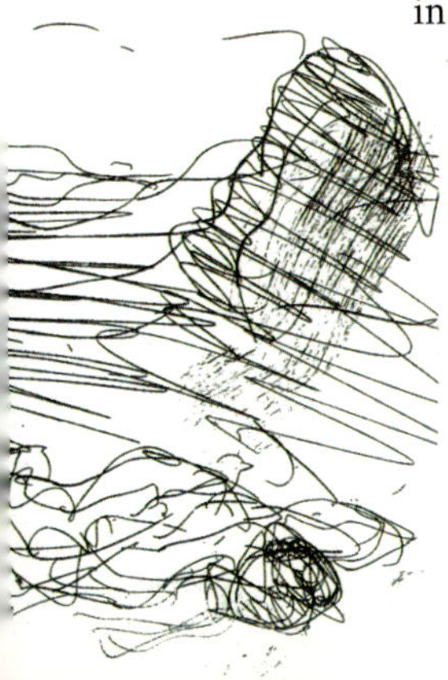

The work also received a favorable review in an article about the Salon in *L'Artiste.* "Like M. Delacroix, M. Corot has discovered how not to resemble his predecessors. This angel in the vast landscape, this far-off hope that the despairing mother does not see, this large landscape; in my opinion, this is a great and noble idea, admirably well executed."

Hagar in the Wilderness placed Corot at the heart of the pictorial movements of his time: the genre of the historical landscape was a product of the classical tradition, while his realistic treatment of trees, rocks and the vast view at the right of the painting attest to Corot's interest—since his return from Italy—in the great seventeenth-century Flemish and Dutch masters. The dramatic and violent subject, the desert theme and the tortured style of the landscape are all signs of Romanticism. The model who posed for the drawing, named "My Hagar" by Corot himself (above), may be a young woman who worked in his mother's shop. According to legend, this would be Alexina Legoux.

Corot at the Salon

Starting in 1835, Corot participated regularly in the Salon, which was the ultimate purpose of his painting. To surprise and seduce the jury, the critics and the public, he alternated his subject matter: after submitting a religious landscape, the following year he entered an antique scene; he then depicted a subject taken from opera or literature, or sent in a "pastoral landscape" inspired from a French or Italian site discovered during his travels. The constant references to classical painting reveal his vast visual and artistic culture and his great loyalty to past master painters.

In 1836, he exhibited two paintings: a "souvenir" of Italy, *View of the Roman Campagna in Winter,* a somber landscape with a Romantic sky; and *Diana Surprised in Her Bath,* influenced by the mythological paintings of the French and Italian Renaissance, and of course, by Poussin. The landscape was inspired by the damp undergrowth of the area around Papigno, as well as by his studies of the Morvan and Fontainebleau forests.
In 1837, Corot, who wanted recognition for his historical compositions, returned to austere landscapes with *Saint Jerome,* conceived as a counterpart to the *Hagar* in the Salon of 1835. The inspiration for the landscape of this stark scene

Corot reused a study made several years earlier in the Rouen Zoo for the lion in *Saint Jerome* (above).

Whether he was painting the solitary and anguished torments of *Saint Jerome* (left), or the more bacchanalian, sweet pleasures of *Silenus* (far left), Corot still drew his inspiration from Nicolas Poussin. The different moods in these two historical landscapes reveal two aspects of the painter's personality: an obvious serenity and *joie de vivre,* which hid a more secret, anxious side. Although the subject of *Saint Jerome* now appears to be traditional and severe, it more effectively transmits the aspirations of an entire generation of Romantics than does *Silenus,* which is an almost joking reference to Poussin and the great classical tradition. This is reflected in the fascination for the painful feelings inherent in human destiny and for violent drama, as well as the desire to fully express these sentiments. *Saint Jerome* was Corot's last attempt—one that was rejected by most critics—at the so-called "severe" religious landscape genre.

—which is reminiscent of the Saint Jerome paintings by Titian and Poussin—came from a trip to the area near Avignon and Montpellier, in Languedoc.

The critics, however, were growing tired of the "austere genre." In 1838, Corot drew on Poussin's bacchanals to paint an amusing *Silenus,* a mythological painting with classical iconography. He also started painting works about dance, in which he could freely express his increasing love of opera, music and ballet.

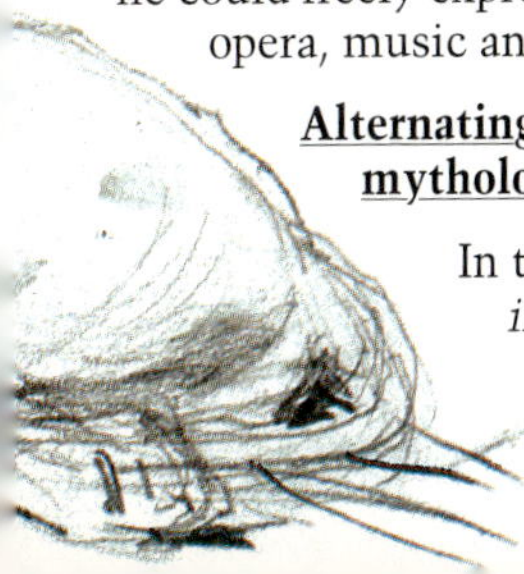

Alternating between mythology and religion

In the Salon of 1840, Corot's *Flight into Egypt,* drawing on a theme from the New Testament, replaced the austerity of the

earlier religious themes with a certain gentleness. The work is said to have been inspired by his friend Parfaite Anastasie Osmond.

That same year, as if by contrast, he exhibited *The Little Shepherd:* this work contains a more personal lyricism, filled with emotion and poetry. His entries for the following year reflected the same search for balance: he presented an atmospheric painting, *View Near Naples,* another Italian "souvenir" containing an elegiacal scene of an Italian peasant dance, along with a more severe painting, *Democritus and the Abderites.* This last work was a tribute to his master Michallon, who had won the Prix de Rome for historical landscape painting with a work on the same subject.

It is striking to note that in 1840, in *The Little Shepherd* (above right), Corot used elements that would become the major themes of his "souvenir" paintings after 1860: a dark ambiance with subtle halftones, cool colors (green and brown), morning or evening light—which created strong contrasts between the shadow and light—and small figures, which were no longer part of a story.

His entries to the Salons of 1842, 1843 and 1844 demonstrate the transitions in his "heroic" landscapes, a theme that had already appeared in earlier Salons. In 1843, the jury refused an ambitious religious landscape, *The Destruction of Sodom,* although Corot was able to enter it the following year. Inspired by the story of the flight of Lot and his family from the city of Sodom, this painting presents an opposing view to the *Flight into Egypt.* Instead of a peaceful depiction of family happiness, this work shows the breakdown of a family. Lot's wife disobeys her husband and is transformed into a pillar of salt because she turned to look back, perhaps in regret, at the city of Sodom consumed by divine anger. The same year, Corot balanced his Salon entry with another important painting devoted to a mythological scene, *The Pastoral Concert,* a synthesis of his love for music and the increasing influence of Titian and Giorgione.

"A man of merit, a conscientious artist who makes every possible effort to find subjects, shapes and appearances that coincide with his vision"

The density and diversity of the paintings he sent to the Salons explain why critics were interested in Corot almost from the first time he participated in the Salon, although professionals viewing his work were troubled by his solitary attitude, as he remained aloof from the aesthetic debates of his time, and Neoclassicists were hesitant about his conception of historical landscape painting.

In *The Orchard* (1842, above), Corot incorporated one of the themes that recurred most frequently in his work: fruit gathering. This required both a modeling technique—for the bodies hanging onto the branches of trees—and a poetic expression of the simple, natural life. The composition of the painting is deliberately asymmetrical: the figures form a triangle on the left side, while the landscape occupies the entire right side.

Corot's development can be seen clearly by comparing *The Little Shepherd* (left) to the work exhibited at the Salon the following year, *Democritus and the Abderites* (far left)—a subject already depicted by Michallon in 1817. The pictorial environment is the same, although the latter work is clearly a historical landscape. Corot was gradually moving from "narrative" paintings to works that primarily depicted feelings.

"The Pastoral Concert"

Two young girls are playing a piece of music in the foreground. Their poses are reminiscent of works by Giorgione and Titian, as well as lesser works, such as the series of muses by Le Sueur. Aside from these clearly classical references, Corot concentrated his landscape skills in this painting. He constructed two distinct sections: one part framed by the plants to the right; and the other leading to the ponds, much like those of Ville-d'Avray. He shaped the tree trunks with precision and added the subtle green of the leaves with small brushstrokes. Painted in 1843 and exhibited the same year as the dramatic *Destruction of Sodom* (following page), *The Pastoral Concert* (left) appears as a sublime prelude to *Morning: Dance of the Nymphs* (1850–51), for its musical theme, and to *Souvenir of Mortefontaine* (1864), which also represented figures gathering fruit, like those in the background of this work. When he altered this work to exhibit it again in the Salon of 1857, Corot considerably reworked the background.

L'INCENDIE DE SODOME.

"The Destruction of Sodom"

As Lot and his family left Sodom, guided by an angel, his wife was transformed into a pillar of salt after turning around for a last look at the city as it was destroyed by God. Older engravings representing the destruction of Sodom are generally faithful to the biblical texts. Inspired by traditional iconography, Corot reversed the usual composition, creating a strong, yet restrained sense of opposing movement: the figures in the foreground move toward the left, while the flames in the distance rise into the air to the right of the building in the background.
Corot used a view of Volterra and a fountain copied in Brittany or Italy for this structure. The overall tone of this painting positioned Corot closer to the Romantic movement than to his Neoclassical training. Refused by the jury for the Salon of 1843, then successfully exhibited in 1844, *The Destruction of Sodom* was entirely reworked in 1857, when Corot submitted it again to the Salon, along with *The Pastoral Concert.*

Corot's historical landscape work, imbued with a particularly rare sense of expression and realism, had many elements in common with the Barbizon school of painters. The champions of modern landscape painting, which appreciated "naiveté," the sincerity of his observation of nature, were disturbed by his constant references to classical painting and by his deliberate and obstinate decision to retain

mythological subjects in his landscapes. "If M. Corot would agree once and for all to kill off all the nymphs that fill his woods, and replace them with peasants, I would love [his work] beyond measure," wrote Zola in 1866. Baudelaire, who advanced his own aesthetic and literary theories in his articles about the Salons, had already used *Homer and the Shepherds* (exhibited in the Salon of 1845) to develop his famous distinction between what is done and what is finished; he claimed

Homer and the Shepherds is one of the last of Corot's classical paintings. Paradoxically, Baudelaire, who was dedicated to defending the new realistic and expressive approach of the Barbizon school of painters, felt that this was a modern work. Corot, however, seemed to have ended an era of his career with this painting. He then developed the theme of the "souvenir."

that a simply sketched work was sometimes more representative of the artist's creativity than a perfectly completed painting.

Yet Corot had achieved success. From this time on, his fellow painters regularly praised his talents and the importance of his work. Indeed,

Delacroix wrote in his *Journal* in 1847 that he had discovered a master in Corot. "Corot is a true artist.... His great *Baptism of Christ* is full of naive beauty. His trees are superb. I spoke to him of the one I have to paint for *Orpheus.* He told me to go beyond myself, to surrender myself to whatever comes.... He does not accept the idea that one can make beauty by taking infinite pains. Titian, Raphael, Rubens, etc., did it easily."

Corot traveled to Switzerland more often than to Italy, going almost every year for long visits to various friends. These included the Leleux and Baud-Bovy families, and the painter Barthélemy Menn, who all loved his work and formed an affectionate circle of admirers around him. He traveled regularly to the banks of Lake Geneva, where he found the same light as in the skies of Italy. The farms, valleys and rural villages in the surrounding countryside reminded him of the Morvan and Burgundy (above, *The Lake of Geneva* below, *Entrance to a Chalet in the Bernese Oberland*).

Rome, fifteen years later

Between May and September of 1843, after the stinging rejection from the Salon, Corot undertook his third and last trip to Italy, this time traveling via Switzerland. By now an experienced painter, he was more interested in producing completed works than simple studies; he therefore painted most of his landscapes directly on canvas. He treated every part of his composition with meticulous detail, while from 1825 to 1828 and even in 1834, he had left the foregrounds unfinished. While he created several masterpieces, including *Tivoli: The Gardens of the Villa d'Este,* he concentrated his research on the treatment of light and shadow.

When Corot visited Tivoli in 1843, he did not depict the famous waterfalls or the picturesque ancient monuments: he preferred instead to paint a panoramic view from the gardens of the Villa d'Este (left). The subtle description of the plants, the bluish tints of the sky and the receding backgrounds make this painting one of the masterpieces of his mature period. As in *"The Raging One"* and his views of Fontainebleau, he placed a figure of a boy looking back at the viewer in the center of the composition. This small peasant, strangely similar to the one in *Boy Wearing a Tall Hat* from Corot's first trip to Italy, appeared in other paintings (such as *Genzano: Goatherd and Village* painted at the same time) and in small, amusing pencil sketches (above).

Corot increasingly concentrated his efforts on an imaginary recomposition of nature and an attentive observation of the relationships between light and volumes, attaching less importance to the theme he was illustrating or the accurate representation of a specific site. He wanted to create a pictorial ambiance and a poetic environment that almost resembled musical abstraction. Describing the atmosphere became the real subject of the painting.

CHAPTER FOUR

THE "SOUVENIR" AND THE QUEST FOR THE GOLDEN AGE (1845–1865)

A horseman crosses a deserted plain (right); several children gather mistletoe from a bare tree (left, detail of *Souvenir of Mortefontaine*). After 1850, Corot's landscapes contained figures in idealized poses, proof that he placed sentiment above all else.

In 1844, on the recommendations of two friends, the publisher Théodore Scribe and the painter Édouard Bertin, Corot was selected by the city of Paris to decorate the baptismal chapel of the Saint-Nicolas-du-Chardonnet Church in Paris. Lengthy discussions with the parish priest were necessary before Corot's subject, the baptism of Christ, was accepted. He carefully prepared each of the figures in the painting by making studies in oil; he then executed one of his most important religious landscapes, which reflects a strong Italian influence. Completed in 1847, the painting was installed in Saint-Nicolas-du-Chardonnet, where it hangs to this day.

Corot began to be accepted by critics and painters, who admired the sincerity of his art as well as his regular participation in the Salons; his first collectors followed soon after and several dealers started to notice his work. Unfortunately, his father, who died in 1847, did not live to see the beginning of his son's professional success. His mother died in 1851. As his family ties became less important and he achieved financial independence, Corot was finally liberated from the constraints that had thus far governed the organization of his life; as a result, he developed strong and loyal friendships.

Friendships with other painters

After 1850, Corot's friendships became increasingly professional. He developed a close relationship with Charles François Daubigny (1817–1878). Starting in 1852, they were often invited to stay with the painter François Auguste Ravier (1814–1895) and together they explored the Dauphiné

When Corot's mother (left) died in 1851, he inherited half of the substantial family fortune, approximately 200,000 *francs-or.* His newfound financial independence grew with the success of his works among collectors. He became close friends with Constant Dutilleux and his two sons-in-law, Alfred Robaut and Charles Desavary (highlighted in sepia, below, in the composite Dutilleux family portrait).

and Isère regions. They also traveled to Switzerland to visit the Baud-Bovy family and Armand Leleux. After 1865, Daubigny regularly invited Corot to his home in Auvers-sur-Oise, where many of his painter friends participated in the decoration of his house.

By 1849, Constant Dutilleux

(1807–1865), a painter and print-maker, seemed to be Corot's closest friend. The two met often, either to work on a motif, or purely for the pleasure of a friendly conversation. Corot shared the joys and sorrows of the Dutilleux family, visiting them once or twice every year starting in 1850; the region of Douai and Arras in northern France became one of his favorite places to study landscapes.

He struck up a friendship with Dutilleux's two sons-in-law, Charles Desavary (1837–1885) and Alfred Robaut (1830–1909), with whom he shared his love of landscapes; in exchange, he received their boundless admiration. Corot chose Dutilleux to accompany him on a trip to Holland in 1854, and it was also Dutilleux who encouraged Corot to take up engraving.

Corot often worked from nature with Constant Dutilleux. The two artists selected a subject and painted side by side, one retouching the work of the other. Dutilleux, an admirer of Delacroix, introduced the two artists. Delacroix praised *The Baptism of Christ* (top left) and Corot gave him a few suggestions about landscape painting.

In 1821, Corot met the mysterious Parfaite Anastasie Osmond, whose husband, the former librarian of the duchesse de Berry, died in 1837. He often visited her in Rosny-sur-Seine and later in Mantes; he seemed to have cared deeply about her.

Drawing and engraving

"Drawing is the first thing to work on," wrote Corot in his youth. "Then, the values—the relationship between the forms and the values. These are the main points. After, the color; and finally, the execution." He grew even more sure of his technical theories with age. He had always sketched; indeed, in Italy he drew more often than he painted in oils. Drawing served at least three different purposes: as a way to remember the forms of nature; as a source of inspiration for imaginary forms that he wanted to capture for later use; and finally, as a preliminary step in the composition of a painting.

In May of 1853, while he was staying in Arras, Dutilleux was struck by Corot's obvious talents as a draftsman and he encouraged his friend to try a new engraving technique invented by two photographers from the north of France: a drawing professor, Cuvelier, and an oil manufacturer, Grandguillaume. Corot liked this medium and produced a total of sixty *clichés-verre* (a glass-negative process) in the years from 1856 to 1860 and from 1871 to 1874.

The spontaneity of his engravings had a lasting effect on his technique. He had become obsessed by the theme of the "souvenir." And a certain decorative mood had gradually entered into his work over the previous few years.

Friends in Mantes

Corot met another of Parfaite Anastasie Osmond's nephews in Rosny-sur-Seine, a man named François Parfait Robert (1814–1875). This brilliant magistrate, who shared Corot's love of Italy, lived in Mantes at the time and regularly invited the artist to visit his home, which was not far from the famous bridge and cathedral of the town. Mantes soon replaced Rosny in Corot's heart. He stayed with the Osmond and Robert families after his great friend Parfaite Anastasie moved to Mantes in 1858.

The historical monuments and the banks of the Seine provided Corot with an infinite source of inspiration. He worked in the surrounding woods (*First Leaves, near Mantes*) and painted the architecture of the town, particularly the strong stone medieval bridge rising from the foliage on the riverbank, dominating the Seine like a fortified castle (a series of *The Bridge at Mantes*), and the Gothic

His passion for drawing, solid constructions and architectural views often lured Corot to the two monuments in Mantes: the cathedral and the bridge (above). A kind of nostalgia, an echo of the romanticism of several paintings from around 1830, appeared more strongly in his work in the 1850s, demonstrated in the poetry of the views of Mantes (far left, *First Leaves, near Mantes*). This nostalgia is even more obvious in the strange self-portrait engraved during this period in the manner of Rembrandt.

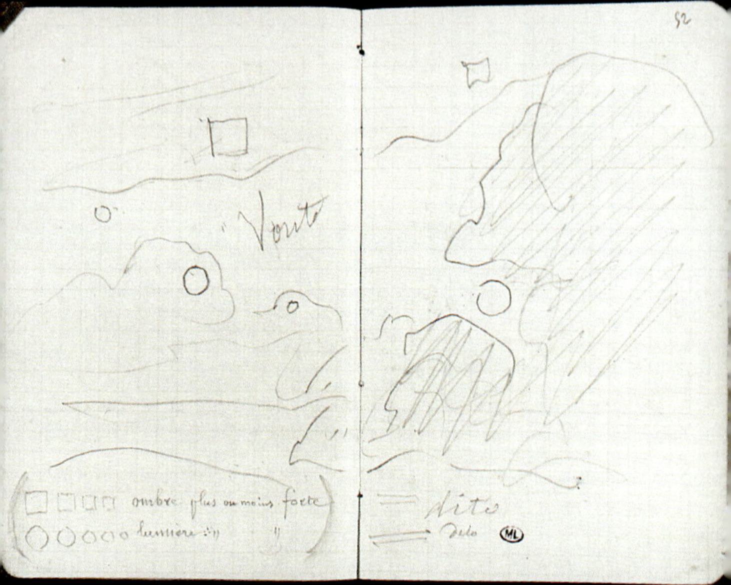
ombre plus ou moins forte
dito

Ce fut à Arras, vers 1848 ou 1850 que Mr Grandguillaume, ancien professeur
de dessin à l'école régimentaire du 3e Génie, qui s'occupait de photographie, et l'artiste
peintre Constant Dutilleux, eurent l'idée de produire un dessin sur verre
rendu opaque, dont on pourrait tirer ensuite des épreuves photographiques.
C. Dutilleux fit les premiers essais vers cette époque et c'est en 1853 qu'il
proposa à Corot de faire un dessin par ce procédé.

Corot tried printmaking as early as 1822, when he made three lithographs (which are now lost). Yet, until 1850, he did not pursue this interest in the medium, while he continued to draw incessantly during his travels. An interesting sketch (far left, top) reveals the graphic techniques he used to take visual notes: symbols—circles and squares—represent shades of light and shadow. The *cliché-verre* technique, a compromise between photography and engraving, reawakened his desire to reproduce his drawings. He again made several lithographs and etchings, although he preferred the *cliché-verre* process when he traveled to northern France. His engravings—quickly drawn, with a spontaneous line—reveal an aspect of Corot's technique that is less visible in his paintings.

cathedral that overlooks the Seine and creates a majestic link between the sky and the water.

Decorative painting

In reply to friendly requests from François Parfait Robert, Corot agreed to paint the walls of his bathroom in 1840. His simple, yet effective decorative project combined the themes of Italy and water. He introduced two major characteristics of the "souvenir" genre that he developed several years later: strong brushstrokes—which he used to improvise from his recollection of an actual site—and a "sentimental," poetic reference to a reinterpreted landscape, which he reconstructed from the vagaries of his memory.

Corot had already created several decorative panels for Théophile Gautier (which have since disappeared). He continued the experience at Ville-d'Avray, where he decorated the summerhouse in his parents' garden with several scenes. He also painted several panels in homes of various friends: the drawing room of the chateau of Gruyères, in Fontainebleau and Magny-les-Hameaux, among others. He also painted four religious views for the church of Ville-d'Avray. And finally, he gave several sketches to his student

The decoration of the Robert bathroom, created during one of his trips to Mantes, is one of the first and most representative examples of Corot's decorative talents. With the exception of the position of the view of Venice (below), located above the window, the various panels are particularly well designed: the subjects are coherent and the arrangement of trees and plants relates to the architectural constraints (bottom left, the gulf of Genoa and gorges in the Tirol; center, the countryside of Naples, Venice and Rome; right, Lake Nemi). Corot's backgrounds were often violently bright, while the foregrounds remained dark. His manner of treating light and the lyricism of his compositions were elegant precursors to the "souvenirs" he developed in his work, especially twenty years later. Fortunately, this decorative ensemble survived the demolition of François Parfait Robert's house in Mantes. Each work, initially painted directly on the wall, was meticulously transferred to canvas.

Oudinot and Daubigny's son, which they used to decorate the Daubigny's house in Auvers-sur-Oise.

Decorative abstraction—which allowed Corot to abandon the idea of a story—and the use of memory were among the essential characteristics of the "souvenir" genre, which occupied a primary place in his work from 1850 on.

The theme of the "souvenir"

Often inspired by a specific site, the Neoclassical landscapes were supposed to be a synthesis of the best parts of this site and above all, of the sensations experienced when studying it. Corot worked alone, in the creative calm of his studio, searching his memory for emotions, feelings and perceptions that he could reintroduce into his various landscapes.

In keeping with his Neoclassical education, Corot composed large mythological subjects,

Corot painted decorative elements for the houses of his friends. He was too old to paint the high walls of Daubigny's house in Auvers-sur-Oise himself, so he asked his student Oudinot to transfer his drawings onto the panels. In tribute, Oudinot decorated a sculpted wood element with a portrait of Corot.

which satisfied his lyrical ambitions through their strongly structured compositions and resemblance to imaginary and marvelous Arcadian landscapes. It is therefore not surprising that the first painting truly created in the spirit of the "souvenirs," *Morning: Dance of the Nymphs,*

and exhibited at the Salon of 1850–51, was a mythological work in the same mood as *Silenus* and *The Orchard.* The classical reference itself plays a less important role than the poetic atmosphere, which is transmitted purely by the landscape; the story has disappeared from the composition.

Morning: Dance of the Nymphs is filled with memories and references. It is clearly reminiscent of Giulio Romano's *Apollo and the Muses,* Mantegna's *Parnassus* and Poussin's *Adoration of the Golden Calf.* This painting was also contemporaneous with *The Golden Age,* a major decorative work painted by Jean-Dominique Ingres for the chateau of Dampierre. In *Morning,* Corot created a new relationship between the mysterious figures frolicking in an idealized landscape and the victorious, omnipresent nature surrounding them.

The main subjects of the "souvenirs" exhibited at the Salons were often highly distorted recollections of Italian views. *Morning: Dance of the Nymphs* (1850) resembles a study painted from the Farnese Gardens in 1826. Corot sometimes reused the same view for later paintings. Lake Garda, painted near Riva in 1834, and already used for a large painting submitted to the Salon of 1835, was again the inspiration for a canvas exhibited at the Salon of 1850–51 (below).

"While seeking a conscientious imitation, I never, even for an instant, lose the emotion that grasped hold of me"

"Beauty in art is truth steeped in the impressions we have received at the sight of nature.... Reality is part of art; feeling completes it," wrote Corot in a notebook in 1855. His aesthetic theories developed

alongside this desire to create a synthesis between what is tangible—the natural forms—and what is intangible—the feeling the artist must communicate to the viewer. "If we have truly been moved, the sincerity of our emotion will be transmitted to others."

The theme of the "souvenir," visible as early as 1840, was completely mastered in *Morning.* It reappeared in the actual title of a painting exhibited in the Salon of 1855, *Souvenir of Marcoussis.* At the same time, Corot submitted a *Souvenir of Italy,* which has disappeared without a trace. And this same word is repeated over and over again: *Souvenir of Ville-d'Avray* in 1857, *Souvenir of the Limousin* (Salon of 1859) and *Souvenir of Italy* in 1861 (three unlocated paintings)—and finally, the famous *Souvenir of Mortefontaine,* exhibited at the Salon of 1864.

Corot still worked fervently on his open-air studies. Each of his trips to one of the French provinces planted the seed for a "souvenir" that could be painted several weeks—or years—after the study.

Just as he reworked the views of Riva in several paintings made after 1850, Corot created several versions of *Morning: Dance of the Nymphs* (above and top left). Although these paintings were often commissions and were executed according to certain commercial considerations, Corot often considerably reworked his copies, making extensive changes in the positions of the group of figures, the orientation of the landscape and even in the poetic effect of the light.

Mortefontaine

The *Souvenir of Mortefontaine* was a decisive development. To the realism and poetry already present in his earlier paintings, Corot added a new compositional style and, especially, a delicate treatment of light, which presaged the "silvery mist" that later became a hallmark of his work.

The park of Mortefontaine is in the Oise *département* north of Paris, where Corot traveled to make several studies. He found the same subtle harmony between the water of the ponds and the overhanging trees as in Ville-d'Avray. But the real aim of the painting was not the pictorial realism, the harvest scene —a theme he treated often, as in *The Orchard*— or indeed any particular story. Corot was trying to transmit a poetic impression, by combining a strong construction with an effect of diffused light.

Maxime Du Camp, writing in the *Revue de Paris,* best summarized the effect of such a work. "The landscapes by M. Corot may not be those that we see, but they are assuredly those that we dream."

Lyricism prevails over realism

The theme of the "souvenir" began to dominate Corot's work. Even the historical landscapes were influenced by

The year 1864 was, after 1859, one of the great moments in Corot's artistic life. He was exhibiting *Souvenir of Mortefontaine* (far left) in the Salon and *The Evening Star* (left) in an important exhibition in Toulouse. Both paintings were purchased immediately, one by the Emperor, the other by the city of Toulouse. These works represent two opposing aspects in Corot's treatment of the "souvenir" genre: *Mortefontaine* depicts an intimate, everyday subject, with the theme of harvesting, while *The Evening Star* is a salute to the evening light, a more lyrical work drawn from the theater and music. This latter painting, inspired by a poem of Alfred de Musset set to music, is a synthesis between the historical landscape genre of his youth and the pastoral paintings of his later years.

In a letter sent to his friend Édouard Brandon, Corot sketched the pond of Mortefontaine (left), the backdrop he intended for a painting he wanted to exhibit at the Salon of 1864. He liked to obtain the opinion of his fellow painters as he developed what he considered to be an important painting.

this new way of working. This is reflected in *Saint Sebastian,* submitted to the Salon of 1853, as well as in such mythological scenes as *The Companions of Diana* (Universal Exposition of 1855), a golden, twilight echo of the silvery, early morning colors of *Souvenir of Mortefontaine.*

The expression of sentiment and lyricism could be even more strongly expressed, and overshadow realism. The works became direct reflections of pure poetry and painting, like music during an opera or a concert. *Bathers with a Child, The Lake* and especially *The Evening Star* deliberately eliminated any connection with actual sites or real topography; they retained only

poetic expression and an evocation of feeling.

At the Salon of 1859, for the first time, Corot masterfully demonstrated his ability to simultaneously treat several themes of a landscape, by means of his "souvenir" system of references. He had finally achieved his goal of fifteen years of research, reflected in the mythological landscape inspired from Dante's *Inferno* (*Dante and Virgile*); in the sensuality of the nude woman in the midst of a landscape taken directly from his studies along the Côte de Grâce (*La Toilette*); and in *Idyll*, or *Hide-and-Seek*, "a piece of countryside in the antique style," in which Corot gave free reign to his pantheist lyricism.

At the 1859 Salon, Corot showed a stark, romantic historical landscape, *Dante and Virgile* (top left), and a sensual, poetic nude, *La Toilette* (above).

The essential role of music

"I interpret with my heart as much as with my eye," Corot declared at this time. This notion of an obvious musical "interpretation" reflects the importance of music and opera in the creation of his landscapes.

Corot had loved opera since his youth. He went to all the Parisian musical events and to concerts two or three times a week. His sketchbooks—which contain the gestures and costumes of opera singers and actors—reflect this love of music. After 1850, music became one of the main sources of inspiration for his work, and musical metaphors appeared often in his paintings. Choreographic poses taken from the opera and pictorial rhythms were like echoes of the concerts. The nymphs, shepherds, and figures in antique costumes seem to come from a musical interlude interrupting an imaginary opera.

Even the composition of his landscapes was affected: in the foreground, figures frolic in front of a curtain of trees, while wide views open out in the background; the figures are skillfully distributed throughout the space of the canvas, as if positioned by a choreographer. The poses of his imaginary figures are reminiscent of the gestures in lyric operas.

Corot (above, his portrait painted in 1858 by Léon Belly) went often to the opera and to concerts in the 1850s. Although he sometimes sketched a musician's gesture in the orchestra pit, he preferred to capture the graceful poses of the dancers who, dressed as nymphs, would later adorn his landscapes.

Realist landscapes

All this obviously had an effect on the real landscapes that Corot continued to paint throughout France. "He does not slavishly copy nature; he makes the trees, with undefined leaves, quiver in a flood of silvery light," wrote Théophile Gautier. A fascinating development! Corot was torn between two temptations: realism, always his absolute priority, and a new interest in poetry, which combined memory and imagination. This duality became more pronounced around 1860. The regions of Mantes, Ville-d'Avray, Marcoussis and Coubron, sketched on site, were reworked at great length in the studio.

The Church at Marissel (above) is typical of Corot's work in the last decade of his life: it is a real landscape, simple, yet beautiful. The views were often quite tame and the artist took many liberties with the topography of the actual site. According to contemporary accounts, the painting was made on site and Corot, dissatisfied with his work and impatient to finish, threw it onto the grass. It is more probable that this canvas was entirely composed in the studio from an open-air study. Queen Victoria was upset that she could not purchase the work in the Salon of 1867, as an ardent collector of Corot's work "beat her to it."

The Church at Marissel, painted in 1866 in a few working sessions while Corot was staying near Beauvais, is surely the most significant example of this distortion of a work painted from nature, in which the painter applied his "souvenir" system to a topographically existing landscape. And Corot, who regularly refused to exhibit open-air studies at the Salon, nevertheless submitted this work to the Salon of 1867.

In the 1860s, Corot made a number of landscapes designed in this manner. He added a few notes of personal poetry to landscapes that were partially painted on site, yet which accurately depicted an existing location. *A Stream near Beauvais, Path under the Trees in Springtime* and *Canteleu, near Rouen* all depict real sites, but they were enriched in the studio through the painter's own memory.

Corot often returned to one particular site in the region of Douai and Arras, perhaps because the play of light in the sky, the reflections in the water and the omnipresent trees reminded him of Ville-d'Avray. This was Saint-Nicolas-lès-Arras, a small village near Arras, where he painted the mill many times from 1865 to his death (below, a version dated 1872). The bell-tower of Saint-Nicolas is visible through a grove of trees (far left, lithograph).

In the spring or late summer, Corot often visited the property purchased by his parents in 1817, where his sister Annette Octavie and her husband often stayed. He found subjects there that were well suited to his work, such as the paths in the hills toward Meudon (left), the famous *The Cabassud Houses* (center) near the family home, and the two ponds (above). He was extermely attached to the village and had created a network of friends among the residents. His open-air study sessions near the ponds attracted many visitors, including the Morisot sisters, who stayed in a nearby hotel so they could watch Corot work.

Corot made portraits from the start of his career and studied life drawing on his first trip to Italy. As he developed his own aesthetic ideas, the role of the figure became increasingly important in his work, soon rivaling his landscape painting. In works of pictorial brilliance, the artist depicted a pose or transmitted a profound emotion.

CHAPTER FIVE
A FLAMBOYANT OLD AGE (1865–1875)

A violence—which had disappeared from Corot's work since *Hagar* and *Saint Jerome* —reappeared in the 1870s in the different versions of *The Gust of Wind* (detail, left), and in the startling witch (right), inspired by Verdi's *Macbeth*.

All the accounts agree: painting from the model was as fundamental to Corot's professional life as were his open-air studies. Moreau-Nélaton wrote that the painter dressed up "one of those working-class women—who were in all the studios—in some kind of Italian-style finery, and set to work for the pleasure of painting, for the joy of capturing a beautiful dark gaze on canvas and harmonizing the white of a blouse with the yellow of a sleeve or red of a skirt." Although he occasionally painted from the model

Corot was still robust and energetic at the time he painted the series of women reading. Without abandoning the landscape genre—indeed, his production increased—he discovered a new inspiration in the female body. Although he always refused to show figure studies, he exhibited *A Woman Reading in the Countryside* (left) in the Salon of 1870. It may be the landscape in the background—a pond, a boat, a fisherman—that convinced Corot to show this work, rather than another study painted in the interior light of his studio.

before 1850, these sessions became more frequent after 1860.

Imaginary figures

The sensuality of the beautiful *Roman Odalisque,* created in 1843 in the studio of the painter Benouville in Rome, shows that for Corot, the relationship between the painter and the model was essential to his study of the figure. He wanted expressive, lively models with whom he could create rich and varied studies. "As for myself, I am not one of those specialists who works in bits and pieces. My purpose is to express life. I need a model who moves," he exclaimed. When Corot worked on a studio composition, he drew on his memory for the sensations he had earlier experienced when working on a specific motif; when painting from the model, however, he was determined to capture the emotion of the moment on the canvas.

While Corot sometimes maintained an ambiguity between portraiture and the imaginary figure, such as in the portrait of *Madame Legois* (1838) or *The Blond Gascon* (ca. 1850), he systematically depersonalized his model after 1860. Moving away from "personality," he concentrated exclusively on universal, almost archetypal attitudes: the woman who dreams, who reads, who observes herself, who contemplates an object or a painting. He created many paintings on the theme of reading (*A Woman Reading, A Woman Reading in the Countryside*). These works allowed Corot to study poses (the young woman with rounded shoulders and bowed head) and to express a dream-like ambiance using a model who—as she concentrates on the written word—seems removed from reality.

Two or three compositions appear over and over again in Corot's figures painted after 1860. One of these is the seated, half-length portrait of *Interrupted Reading* (left), in which the model gazes at the viewer against the backdrop of the studio, or the *Woman Reading in the Countryside* (far left) and *Melancholy. A Woman Reading with a Velvet Skirt* (above), however, is one of the rare paintings with a standing figure, framed from a distance. Absorbed in her reading, the young woman is placed in a natural setting.

Indeed, Corot invented an entirely personal variation on this theme, that of interrupted reading, in which the model, suddenly disturbed in her calm activity, reestablishes an uneasy contact with reality and observes the viewer with a gaze that still seems lost in the emotion of her book. This gentle daydreaming soon became a subject in itself, as in such paintings as *Melancholy* and *Meditation.*

Corot brought back a jumble of costumes and accessories from Italy and used them to dress up his models. He was particularly fond of two or three types of regional outfits: Italian, Albanian and Oriental. The Greek tunic, worn (bottom left) by one of his favorite models, Emma Dobigny—whom he liked for her fresh, natural personality during long hours of work—recurs frequently in works from this period. The beautiful Moorish dress, worn by the model in *Algerian Woman* (top left) —perhaps borrowed from a friend—was only used once.

Nudes and disguises

Corot filled his studio with all kinds of accessories, as well as regional and theatrical costumes. He used them according to his mood of the moment, and they formed both the pretext and the subject for the painting. "She was no longer Mariette, Clémence or Emma. She was the Naiad, the Bacchante or the Muse; she was the nymph Eurydice and the priestess Veleda," wrote Moreau-Nélaton. Corot used the sessions—in theory devoted to the study of the human body—to create paintings that were still evocative, but drew their charm, strength and identity from the description of a regional costume or antique subject. Art historians and biographers have considered the

theme of the nude to be of minor importance —although it was a recurring subject—in Corot's work. This position is indefensible, in that all these studies were based on a love of the female body that equaled his passion for nature.

Below (*The Woman with the Pearl*), an ironic reference to Leonardo da Vinci's *Mona Lisa* or to certain portraits by Raphael.

Corot, first and foremost a landscapist, nevertheless was often drawn to one of the favorite subjects of history painters: the nude. Like an amateur exploring a field that was not his own, Corot hesitated between serious classicism and the humor of his time in various masterfully painted studies in this genre. Although *Repose* (bottom left) seems to be influenced by Giorgione or Titian, he added a small troop of mythological drinkers in the background, in a manner closer to Poussin's style. The pictorial treatment of *Bacchante with a Panther* (top right) —reflecting a fondness for the supernatural and the grotesque—is similar to works made thirty years earlier by the Romantics, at the time Corot was decorating Théophile Gautier's apartment. In both these paintings, despite some clumsiness in the anatomical treatment, or rather the deliberate foreshortening (indeed, this so disturbed Ingres that he refused to make any comment, so as not to hurt Corot's feelings), he painted the female body with an extreme sensuality.

Success

As he grew older, Corot was increasingly obliged to satisfy the entreaties of dealers and collectors who fought over his work, including the figure paintings. On July 5, 1846, he was named *chevalier* of the French Legion of Honor, then *officier* in 1868. Yet never, not even in the last year of his life, did he receive the first-class medal from the Salon, an official recognition certainly warranted by his long and productive career. To correct this insult, his friends presented Corot with their own medal during a memorable evening organized on December 29, 1874, in the Grand Hôtel in Paris.

In Corot's last years, the studio on the rue du Faubourg Poissonnière was not only his favorite place to workbut it was also his house where he received many of his friends. The works from his early years and the unsold Salon paintings drew dealers and collectors. Corot had a studio made in Coubron (above) where he could paint in calm and solitude.

As a result of his increasing public success, Corot had to deal with an unending stream of commissions for works that were often similar in nature. By this time he had assistants helping with his landscapes. Although he did not create a real studio, in the sense of a workshop, he nevertheless delegated certain tasks to a few students who had assimilated particularly well his technique. And when he wanted time to create a few paintings with a more personal pictorial treatment or subject, he took refuge with friends in Coubron, to the south of Paris, or at 19 bis, rue Fontaine in Paris, two studios that were less encumbered with students, dealers, collectors and petitioners of all sorts.

Corot created an affectionate description of his everyday life by posing a model in front of an easel that held a landscape in progress. Six studies depict his studio, including the model holding a mandolin, under the indifferent gaze of *The Blond Gascon* (below), and the deeply melancholic model with a small book still in hand (far left).

"A feeling for the movement of things"

Success and its attendant concessions did not prevent Corot from trying to achieve an ultimate synthesis in his pictorial

concerns. By 1870, his works were less analytical in construction. On a formal level, he concentrated on the overall values, while depicting the diffuse sentiment of nature. "I try to render the quivering of nature.…When looking at my canvas, which does not, in fact, move, I want the viewer to have a feeling for the movement of things." He still traveled as much as ever and exhibited every year in the Salon. This desire to renew his art, which lasted

through his old age, resulted in some of his greatest masterpieces. *The Road to Sin-le-Noble,* probably painted on site during a trip to the Douai region, reveals a painter who had totally integrated the spontaneity and realism of the seventeenth-century Dutch and Flemish painters. Yet Corot's ultimate aesthetic statement is best expressed in *Interior of the Sens Cathedral* and *The Belfry, Douai.*

Corot feared radical changes: he painted *The Belfry, Douai* after leaving the upheaval of the Paris Commune, taking refuge in Arras and Douai with his two friends Desavary and Robaut. It contains the same freshness, the same inventive observation, as his studies of Chartres Cathedral painted forty years

Corot discovered the poetry of the towns of northern France when visiting the Dutilleux family. He painted *The Belfry* (above) in Douai and became fond of *The Road to Sin-le-Noble* (left), on the outskirts of the town.

earlier. He adopted the same colors as the seventeenth-century Dutch painters in his treatment of the stones and roofs, and created the same contrast of clouds and transparency as in the northern skies. Very different from the dark halftones of his Salon paintings, this *Belfry* reflects the instinctual sense of light that Corot had always possessed.

Realism or objectivity

Light does not always mean pale colors, nor does realism always imply objectivity, or an imitation of nature. Corot avoided sudden changes in both art and politics. This explains his uneasy attitude toward the younger Impressionist generation. He was scared of the strong social demands in works by Millet and Courbet, but at least their technical language was similar to his own.

The Impressionists, however, added a technical rebellion to the revolution in subject matter. Corot refused to vote for Manet in a Salon jury, preferring his colleague Isabey, but he did, have several students who were associated with the group of Impressionists, including Pissarro, the Morisot sisters, Chintreuil and Stanislas Lépine.

Corot influenced Impressionism, although unintentionally, through his study of light and the realistic spontaneity of his painting technique. But because he valued the artist's sensibility and the expression of his imagination, he had a stronger effect on the Symbolist movement, and even Cubism.

The many commissions and his increasing preoccupation with the figure did not deter Corot from his passion for depicting architecture. When painting *Interior of the Sens Cathedral* (below), he experienced the same emotions, reinforced by the beauty and luminosity of the stained-glass windows, as he had in Venice in 1834, where he had painted the interior of

the San Marco Basilica. He mixed an astonishing range of whites and yellows to paint the columns and the arches, and to emphasize the intense red and blue of each window. This work remains the ultimate masterpiece among his architectural subjects.

The Gust of Wind (above) was clearly begun with the desire to explore a new theme: the expression of untamed nature. There were several variations; indeed forgers used it systematically. A relatively marginal theme in his work, it is nonetheless an interesting demonstration of a sentimental vision of nature as depicted by Corot.

Upon a base of Neoclassical experience, he constructed a body of work so varied that it was able to influence a diverse group of artists.

"Spry and cheerful old man"

He still had an astonishing amount of energy in 1872. "It appears as if, in reward for his unwavering love of Nature, M. Corot

received in return a mysterious gift of rejuvenation. Age has no effect on the vigor of this spry and cheerful old man. Work seems to increase his energy," wrote one amazed critic. This vigor radiates from his last figures: *Monk with a Cello*—his ultimate metamorphosis of a theme that recurred throughout his work since Italy—and the unsettling *Lady in Blue,* an emotional condensation of all the painter's research in the domain of imaginary figures.

The last years of Corot's life brought the final proof of his success: his work was imitated and copied —and forgeries began to appear. Although for commercial reasons Corot seemed to repeat variations on the same theme, he nevertheless persisted with his personal and innovative work, as demonstrated by the last paintings exhibited at the Salon, *Byblis* and *Woodcutter's Wives.* Far from the "souvenirs" that ensured his success, Corot returned to the realistic and luminous landscapes of his youth. And the imaginary figures of his last ten years offer a new aesthetic viewpoint, somewhere between pure painting and poetic expression—an outlook that also touched the sensibilities of twentieth-century painters.

"More rose-colored, deeper, more transparent!"

Despite his fame and commercial success, Corot continued his research. Faced with the difficulty of such work, and when nature resisted and refused to be apprehended by the human spirit, he applied his

It is significant that during the last months of his life, while contemplating nature and forms, Corot—despite many commercial demands —became interested for the first time in a realistic and sensual theme he had never treated before: still-lifes, the most of subjects (*Bouquet,* 1874, above, middle).

unvarying principle, that "one must not allow indecision in a single thing."

He was deeply affected by the death of his sister Annette Octavie Sennegon. A short time before he died, on February 22, 1875, he started to have self-doubts. As he lay suffering an illness of his digestive system, he expressed his thoughts to Alfred Robaut, a frequent visitor to his apartment-studio on the rue du Faubourg Poissonnière. "I glimpse things I have never seen before. It seems to me that I never knew how to paint a sky! What I see before me is much more rose-colored, much deeper, more transparent!" To the end of his days, his Neoclassical legacy left him with an obsession for the skies that he had copied incessantly when he was still learning his craft—how to render this "rose color more transparent"?—and with the patient introspection of memory that allowed the artist to create imaginary worlds from his visual experience.

Lady in Blue (above) could be seen either as a straightforward portrait of a friend or a more general expression of mood. The model gave him a pictorial pretext to describe the contrast between her white arm and the delicate fabric in a setting created by the strength and sensuality of the image.

DOCUMENTS

The biographers

In 1905, Alfred Robaut and Étienne Moreau-Nélaton published the Catalogue raisonné *of Corot's work. The paintings, drawings and prints are classified systematically and chronologically in a four-volume set. For the first time in art history, each work—represented either by a photograph or a drawing—includes a description or precise historical information.*

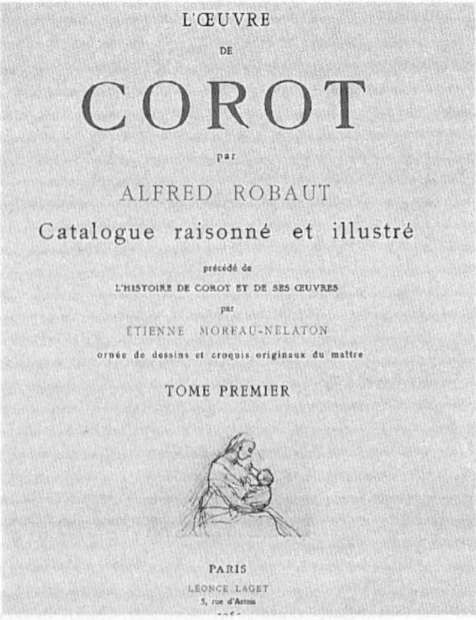

L'ŒUVRE

DE

COROT

par

ALFRED ROBAUT

Catalogue raisonné et illustré

précédé de

L'HISTOIRE DE COROT ET DE SES ŒUVRES

par

ÉTIENNE MOREAU-NÉLATON

ornée de dessins et croquis originaux du maître

TOME PREMIER

PARIS

LÉONCE LAGET

5, rue d'Artois

Alfred Robaut (1830–1909)

Son of a printer-engraver from northern France, Alfred Robaut was born in Douai in 1830 into a family where art held a place of honor. On May 16, 1853, he married the daughter of Corot's great friend, the painter Dutilleux, who taught Robaut painting and lithography.

He soon abandoned original engraving and worked instead on reproduction engraving.

Robaut took over his father's printing plant in 1853, although he kept his job, as the official artist-designer for the Commission of Regional Antiquities in the Pas-de-Calais, a position he had taken up in 1852. He had become close friends with Corot and in 1872 he moved from Arras to Paris to be closer to the painter.

An art historian and artist, Robaut was also a talented man of letters. He wrote numerous articles, which were published in such magazines as *L'Art, L'Art français, La Galerie contemporaine, L'Illustration, Le Journal des Arts* and *Le Monde illustré.*

Robaut greatly admired Delacroix, and his career as an art historian began with the publication in 1885 of the *Œuvre complet de Delacroix,* with text by Ernest Chesneau; Robaut engraved all the reproductions of the painter's works.

He died on April 8, 1909, in Fontenay-sous-Bois, east of Paris, four years after the publication of the *Catalogue raisonné.*

Étienne Moreau-Nélaton (1859–1927)

Étienne Moreau-Nélaton was born in Paris in 1859 into a bourgeois family, where art was at least as important as in the Robaut family. Indeed, the collection of his grandfather, Adolphe Moreau, was famous during the Second Empire.

While attending the prestigious École normale supérieure, he also studied painting, first with Henri Harpignies, then with Albert Maignan. He exhibited for the first time at the Salon of 1884, finally earning his status as a painter nine years after Corot's death. His work, virtually unknown today, was strongly influenced by Impressionism.

He only started collecting paintings and studying art history seriously after the death of his wife and one of his daughters in a fire at the *Bazar de la Charité.* He collected close to one hundred canvases by nineteenth-century masters, including works by Daumier, Delacroix, Géricault, Fantin-Latour, Manet, Monet, Sisley, Puvis de Chavanne and, of course, Corot. Most of his collection, including the finest pieces, are now in French museums, thanks to a series of donations (in 1906, 1907 and 1919) and to a large bequest (in 1927) after his death.

One author takes over from the other

We do not know how he and Robaut met. Étienne Moreau-Nélaton merely wrote a short explanation in the preface to the catalogue. "It is unimportant to know what destiny led me to offer my services and substitute my good intentions for his knowledge.... But he was getting older and tired, and gradually, the courageous worker, whose strength was failing, had lost hope of finishing a project that had become too much for him."

In the 1860s, Alfred Robaut started collecting documents and descriptions of Corot's life and works; he never missed an opportunity to obtain an anecdote about the master's life or a reminiscence of something he said. But he didn't stop there: he drew or asked his brother-in-law, Charles Desavary, to photograph every work by Corot he could get his hands on. And in August 1872, he even moved 600 works from Corot's studio to Arras where Desavary could photograph them more conveniently. Finally, he dated the works, often with Corot's approval.

Thanks to this documentary undertaking, we have an extremely precise idea of the early stages of certain paintings—which were often either considerably modified by Corot, or disfigured for unknown reasons.

Étienne Moreau-Nélaton took a real interest in this project only after Corot's death, and purchased all the paintings and documents he could find. As Robaut was too old to write the text for the catalogue, Moreau-Nélaton began this task during the winter of 1902, working on the project every winter until 1905. He annotated, classified, wrote and gathered the documents that Robaut had started collecting in the mid-nineteenth century (most of these are now in the collections of the Bibliothèque nationale and the Louvre Museum). He discussed this project in his *Mémorial de Famille.*

Charles Desavary (above) took close to 600 photographs of Corot's paintings: far left, a first version of the *Concert;* below, as it is today (altered in 1857).

"February [1902]: I have undertaken the publication of the catalogue of Corot's work prepared by Alfred Robaut; all the documents of this project are now in my hands. I will spend three winters on this work. I will penetrate into the intimate world of the master. I will write 'the history,' as an introduction to the 'catalogue' of his work."

"1903: January–May. Preparation of my 'history of Corot' and creation of the catalogue of his work from the documents provided by Alfred Robaut."

Alfred Robaut made drawings of a great many of Corot's paintings. *Soissons Seen from Mr. Henry's Factory* (left) and *Diana Surprised in Her Bath* (above) reveal his talent. These drawings were accompanied by notes summarizing the history of each work, from its creation to the various owners. Right, Corot's room in February of 1875.

"1904: January–May. Wrote the text for the 'history of Corot'; printing has begun, which will be followed by the printing of the catalogue of his work, to continue throughout the rest of the year."

"1905: January. Publication of 'Corot's work,' preceded by the 'history of Corot.'"

Four hundred copies of this four-volume catalogue—now out of print—were published by Floury.

Gérard de Wallens

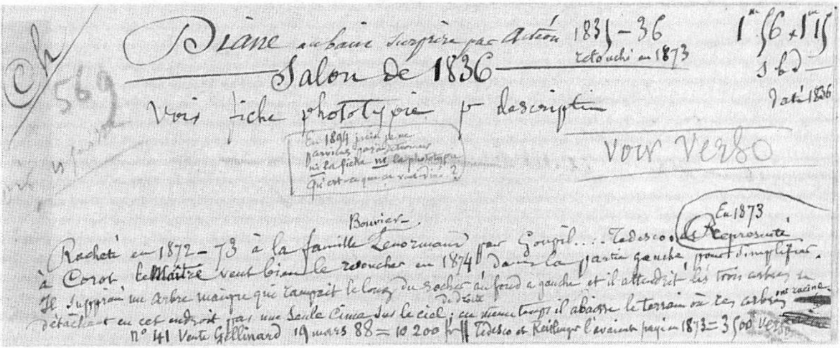

Corot by Corot

In 1924, when Étienne Moreau-Nélaton republished Corot's voluminous catalogue, he used original sources —notebooks, letters to his family and friends, and verbal descriptions— to describe the man and his work, and decided to title it Corot by Corot.

Most of Corot's letters (many of which have since been acquired by the Department of Graphic Arts, Louvre Museum, and the Department of Prints, Bibliothèque nationale) were collected by Alfred Robaut and Étienne Moreau-Nélaton.

As opposed to Eugène Delacroix or Edgar Degas, Corot was not overly candid in his letters. Aside from the letters written in his youth to Abel Osmond—which are among the most intimate and the only ones that allow a real glimpse into his personality—most of his letters are short and to the point: he discusses a trip, the acquisition of a work or the payment of a transaction.

Letters to Abel Osmond from Rome

Rome, March 1826

My dear friend,

First of all, I want to tell you that your letter gave me a great deal of pleasure. Our epistolary exchanges always take me back to Paris and allow me to feel almost all its pleasures. I have to seriously concentrate on my great need to persevere in my work to have separated myself like this from my good friends. I am no longer a part of those good evenings. We can no longer meet for those gentle rendezvous on the rue du Bac for the four of us. Well, you are surely still going there. Please, from time to time, tell those ladies that "Camille is dreadfully sorry that he can't come this evening; but it is certainly not pleasure that keeps him away, as it is only with you that he finds any." Tell them this a little bluntly, just as I would....

Is Corot writing? He is more likely to be sketching in this detail of a watercolor painted by Daumier around 1850.

Finally, my poor Abel,
I promise I will work
during my trip to Italy,
so as not to be ashamed
of expatriating myself
for so long in order
to bring back nothing.
As for myself, I will be
very happy on my
return. I foresee the
delight in the place
I will be: this renews
my energy. Once
back in France,
I will certainly miss
the beautiful country of
Italy, but at least I will
have glimpses of it in my studio.
I will have portraits so that I can still
visit the region. Thank you very
much for your contribution to the
toast in my honor....
Adieu, much love, and I beg to
apologize for all the pain I have caused
this friendly and tireless messenger
of friendship. But his zeal reassures
me. I would like to tell him: see
you tomorrow. But that will come,
let's hope.
Adieu, from the one who loves you,
(Louvre Museum, Department of
Graphic Arts, AR 8 L3)

Rome: The Coliseum Seen Through Arches of the Basilica of Constantine.

Rome, May 1826

You figured me out. Even though
I suffered at the lateness of your
letter, I have forgiven you considering
the pleasure it gave me. I curse
the rheumatism pains that are torturing
such a zealous messenger as you
are. It was really too nice of you to have
run my little errands so punctually.
I consider myself lucky, exiled
as I am, to have a friend like yourself,
who is kind enough to send me
news of Paris and of what I miss there.
Ah! That is so much like my mother,
worrying about the attention
I paid to the young Saint L. ladies...
I was well aware of her torments
and I think that, in terms
of the consequences she dreaded,
my departure must have reassured
her a great deal; I am somewhat
too far away now to arouse her
fears.... My dear Abel, I know that
you will always be there to render
service. Your helpful advice, telling
me to send a letter to Mlle Anna
is proof of that. But I foresee
a problem: it's just that if, as you
suggest, I disguise my handwriting, she
herself will be deceived, and her
surprise, which could be revealed in
the midst of those ladies, could reveal
the subterfuge, something we must
avoid. So, I am putting myself in your
hands: figure out a way, when you
talk to her, to tell her that a poor devil,
exiled in the Papal states, is always
thinking of his *formosa* Dido.
It's probably your rheumatism that
has prevented you from seeing
my mother and father for so long.
When my prayers are answered

and your pain alleviated, go see them; kiss them for me....

I gave your message to Behr and he asks me to thank you for remembering him. We are always together. We are about to leave on a trip. By the second Wednesday of the month, we'll no longer be in Rome. Until I have a chance to send something better to Mlle Anna, can you give her this small piece of antique glass I'm sending with this letter? It is not very valuable, but at least it has the merit of being old. You can give it to her before you tell her you received a letter from me.

Behr just gave me half of an orange. I hope you can enjoy one just as delicious. In the meantime, I send you all my love. Write to your loyal friend.

Camille

(Louvre, DGA, AR 8 L4)

"I have only one aim in life, which I want to pursue steadfastly; to make landscapes"

Papigno, August 8, 1826

From the depths of a thick forest with the background noise of the waterfalls, I want to assure you, my good Abel, that in no way did I accuse you of negligence. My mother and my sister both informed me of your illness. Far from being mad at you, I felt for you with all my heart. Will these damnable pains not leave you alone? I will talk to the Holy Father: this must stop, as this rheumatism is making two suffer. I understand your letter clearly, but despite that, I did notice that the handwriting was not as steady as in earlier letters. I am well aware of the efforts you are making.

Ah, you rogue! You saw those ladies after two months of illness; and me, I have not seen them in nine months of good health. It seems to me that from now on, it's my turn to suffer courageously. I am somewhat comforted to learn that they are all well. Is Mlle Alexina really happy? I reproached myself enormously for my poor choice in the rosary. I have since seen some that she would have liked; but it's done.

...But after all, my friend, I liked Mlle A. a great deal and I still do. But I have only one aim in life, which

I want to pursue steadfastly; to make landscapes. This firm resolution will not allow any serious attachments. By this I mean marriage. As for my little love, I can assure you that, once back in Paris, if I am allowed to kiss her from time to time, I could reconcile myself with my celibacy. I still love that young lady; but my independent nature and the serious study, for which I feel a great need, mean that I will treat *the thing* as a laughing matter. Ecco....

The forest of Ville-d'Avray is still there to welcome the swarm of lovely young ladies. Go, go romp around under the leaves of the strong oak tree and the melancholy birch. Above all, be careful with your straw hat, if it still survives. Remember how we used to fill it up with a good portion of the bad lunch from Ezéchiel....

If you're not in pain and you reply quickly, you can take credit for making your loyal friend happy.

(Louvre, DGA, AR 8 75)

Letter to François Parfait Robert

This letter, filled with memories that Corot wanted to share with his friend Robert as he traveled through Italy, reveals one of the main reasons for the friendship between the two men: their mutual love of the Mediterranean coast. We do not know if it was written before Corot painted the decoration for Robert's bathroom.

Paris, April 5, 1840

My dear Robert,

...I have had news of you: I was present when your last letter from Naples was read; it appears that you are delighted with this beautiful country. What a beautiful sky! This gulf is so magnificent! What a site, the Capo di Monte! And the promenade along the riva Santa Lucia, from which you can see the islands of Capri and Ischia, which you probably visited. We will have a great talk about it on your return; I would like that and it will refresh my dwindling memories.

So you are in Rome, a city unmatched for the austerity and grandeur of its design. Walk along the Pincio and in the Farnese Gardens, along the Campo Vaccino. Study the physiognomy well so that you can tell me when you get back if I have properly rendered this grand and austere scenery. Don't forget to make a few trips by *caratella* into the Roman countryside, along the banks of the Tiber up to Ponte Mole. You have enough time to get a good idea of this beautiful city and the surrounding countryside. You must also visit Tivoli and Monte Cavo, and Albano, Frascati, Grotta Ferrata, Marino and Nemi. In Marino ask for Sorra Marta, who runs an inn, and send her lots of good wishes from a Frenchman who stayed with her in 1827 and who was there one year earlier with two other painters, one of whom had a limp.

I gave you the names of Bodinier and Buttura, a *pensionnaire* at the Academy. Have you seen them? Please send them my best regards, as well as to a young man named Jardin, whose address you can get at the Caffè Greco, via de' Condotti, who was kind enough to write me a letter I intend to answer soon. Have a good time, see a lot and good health to you both. My compliments to Madame Robert.

The Salon has just reopened. My *Flight into Egypt* was placed in the Salon Carré; it's famous!

(cited by Rodolphe Walter, in Archives de l'Art français, T XXVIII)

Letter to Constant Dutilleux

Starting in 1847, the affectionate correspondence maintained with Constant Dutilleux seemed to be an exception to his other letters: the friendship between the two men allowed Corot to reveal himself freely.

Paris, January 24, 1849

Sir,

Your letter gave me a great deal of pleasure. I thank you very much for reiterating your invitation to come visit. Rest assured, Sir, that even if it is only for a few days, I look forward to making this short trip when the weather turns nice. I showed your letter to my mother who, after what you wrote, will have to give me the freedom to rush to see you. And together, we can take a few moments to admire this wonderful scenery, which reveals its beauty and delight to any man who seeks it. Long live knowledge and simplicity! It is the only path that leads to what is true and sublime. I am working hard on the painting of Christ. I hope it will come; it has changed a lot since you saw it. I still see things to take out so as to make it look as simple as possible. The people who come to my studio generally seem to like it. I will probably have the pleasure of seeing you at the Exposition, if we are to have one.

I'm looking forward to seeing you in Paris or in Arras, yours most sincerely....

(Bibliothèque nationale, Department of Prints)

"We will have a good time making masterpieces"

Boulogne-sur-Mer, September 2, 1857

My dear friend,

I have been in Boulogne since yesterday and will stay until the twelfth, when I plan to join you in Arras and embrace all of you. Isn't Colin supposed to join our excursion to Dunkirk? We will have a good time making masterpieces, which will console us for our problems about the exhibition. I was only able to find one of your paintings; the others, it seems, were poorly placed; we will talk all about it. A short time ago, I sent a small painting to M. Legentil. He was kind enough to let me know it arrived and tells me he is happy with it. Apparently, a shoulder needs to be reworked; we'll see about that and will comply with the opinion of the Areopagus.

Yours, and with a handshake.

(Bibliothèque nationale, Department of Prints)

In the forest of Fontainebleau

Corot occasionally lived in a house near the forest of Fontainebleau that belonged to his friend Philippe Comairas (1803–1875), who was one of Ingres' students.

Paris, January 7, 1852

Sir,

Philippe told me that you would prefer to have a souvenir of trees from me, rather than a study of buildings. Together, we selected a view of Saint Peter and the Castel Sant'Angelo. According to your letter, we looked in the studio. We selected a study of trees made at Ville-d'Avray. I have indicated the specific aspects below, and you can choose and tell us which one you prefer in your next letter, so we can order the frame as soon as possible.

I would be delighted to see something of mine that you like in your house. I'll take advantage of this opportunity to thank you for the warm welcome you gave me when I went through your town. We often speak of it with Philippe. Don't forget to give my regards to Mlle Silette.

Yours sincerely.

(Louvre, DGA, AR 8 L18)

"I do, in fact, have some elms for him."

The following letter was sent to Swiss painter Armand Leleux, who around 1850 was one of Corot's great friends. The painter frequently stayed with Leleux near Geneva and it was through him that Corot met the Bovy family and Barthélemy Menn.

My dear Armand,

I will definitely arrive Monday evening or Tuesday morning. I saw Strotton, with whom I would be delighted to deal, provided he makes me acceptable offers.

These art dealers are stupid. They buy landscapes, but on condition that they be as remote from nature as possible. But I would never be able to make a landscape that wasn't really one. I cannot manage to depict trees in any way other than how they grow, no more than a headless man, without a trunk or legs. The ways things are going, perhaps this is the future. We will see soon enough. But while Strottin waits for my new style, I do, in fact, have elms available for him.

Regards to you and your dear wife.

(cited in the press and dated 1863)

Birdsong and man-made storms

The suffering that Corot discusses in this letter sent to La Rochenoire probably refers to the war and the Commune, which compelled him to leave the capital for Arras.

Paris, February 14, 1871

My dear friend,

How I thank you for your thoughtfulness and your concern over our fate this winter. Oh yes! We did indeed suffer. Health is good. I hope, like you, that we can see each other soon. So, there are exhibitions of paintings over there? Why, only seven hours apart, are two countries treated so differently? This is something I simply cannot understand. Yet I will tell you, so that you don't worry, I have never had so much energy for work. I am producing more this winter than I usually do. I think that misfortune has forced me to take refuge under the vault of the sky and the thick clouds, and to position myself as best as I can to listen to the birdsong. Compared with that and the calm, what do man-made storms matter? Long live the falling stars in the month of July and the pretty small flowers in the fields!
I am happy to hear that all three of you are in good health, as well as the Daubigny family. Apparently my painting is getting established in England: let's be happy!

Audry and all the friends are well.

All the best,

Kiss the ladies for me.

(quoted by Moreau-Nélaton in 1905)

Forgeries: true or false?

"Corot painted 3,000 paintings; 10,000 of them have been sold in America." This famous line, written in 1936, refers to a notorious scandal concerning 2,144 forged paintings, and only partially explains the questions surrounding the Corot fakes.

Portrait of Camille Corot by Jules Guédy.

Corot, of course, is not the only artist whose work has been forged, but he is a rarity in that he contributed, willingly or not, to the creation of fake versions of his pictures.

The forgers' good fortune

It is difficult to sum up the subject of Corot forgeries in a few lines without over simplifying the question. Nevertheless, the fact that Corot painted nearly 3,000 canvases is essential to any understanding of this issue. Among this large number of works, which in itself encouraged a certain amount of malpractice, a fair quantity were replicas or copies made by Corot himself. He often returned to a particular painting and modified it in various ways (an unhoped-for source of inspiration for the forgers) to satisfy a commission or for his own artistic research. Finally, and this is the crux of the matter, Corot believed that he was the author of the idea and not of the painting itself. It was this conviction that led him to sign pictures, that he had not painted or had only partially worked on, and he was all the more willing to do so if he thought it would help someone who was down on his luck. Indeed, Corot was well known for his generosity.

The difficulties of authentification

Corot, however, is not fully to blame. Several generations of art historians have contributed to the proliferation of forgeries by incorrect attributions. In addition, many paintings by his friends, pupils and followers were "transformed" and after the death of the artist a veritable forgery industry spread across Europe and the United States. The practice tailed off during the 1920s and today researchers are sorting through this body of work to study it, which has rarely been done before.

The relatively large quantity of forged works should not be allowed to tarnish Corot's reputation, and he remains one of the greatest nineteenth-century French artists. Nor should this prejudice the search for several fine works which may still come to light, either because they have been lost or because they have been kept in private collections.

Investigative Methods

Aesthetic analysis is quite often the only method used to attribute a work of art, whether it be an object or a graphic work. Researchers make their judgements on the basis of their own knowledge of the work of a particular artist or school. This method is usually satisfactory and is, in any case, good enough to dismiss insignificant works. But these empiric and subjective methods no longer meet the exacting demands of art history and archeology.

There are at least four major categories of methods used to back up a rigorous investigation: auxiliary sciences (dendrochronology, palynology, paleography), research publications which are available in libraries, archives (original documents) and laboratory analysis (physical, chemical, radiological). It is through their combined use that researchers establish "objective" criteria for the attribution of each type of work; numerous investigators now work in this way today.

Attribution: an example

The following case offers an example of this approach, applied, with limited means, to a picture discovered by chance and analyzed at the *Laboratoire d'étude des œuvres d'art par les méthodes scientifiques* at the University of Louvain.

General view of the painting and frame. At first glance, it easily passes as one of a series of works produced by Corot.

The first, purely formal analysis (including the frame) is done with the naked eye. The researcher systematically notes the pictorial artistry: the colors, the forms, the composition, the signature and the back of the canvas. All the marks or inscriptions which could direct

A detail showing a section of the buildings on the left-hand side of the painting: certain isolated elements of the work could easily be attributed to Corot.

Detail of the figure in the foreground. Corot nearly always depicted one or more such figures. They are among the classic elements of his work. Forgers have rarely understood their significance and have difficulty reproducing the poetic and meditative sentiment that Corot gave to them.

The information on the back of a picture is often suspect, as it is easy to fake and can misleadingly strengthen an attribution. Collectors, on the other hand, consider this type of information to be very important.

the investigator to further areas of research are also assessed.

The information is compared with what is known of the picture's provenance and history. Usually, this entails a certain amount of research in libraries and archives.

During this first stage the picture is taken to a laboratory where various technical analyses are performed, such as radiography, reflectography, observation under ultraviolet light and under a microscope (using varying lights). As a general rule, all the research stages, including infrared examination involve photography.

From the microscope to the X-ray

The examinations under the microscope and under ultraviolet light (not illustrated) add depth to the information gained from the first observations made with the naked eye. In the present example, the ultraviolet investigation reveals that some modifications were made to the picture's composition after the painting was finished, and that the signature has been tampered with. The microscope clearly confirms this: the signature was added some time after the painting was completed, and has left a residue of black paint at the bottom of some of the deep cracks in the picture.

Thanks to the absence of paint in places, the structure of the pictorial layers can be closely studied. Other less important observations are noted, some of which will be made clearer by X-ray examination. For example, the white spot, clearly visible in the tree on the right-hand side of the

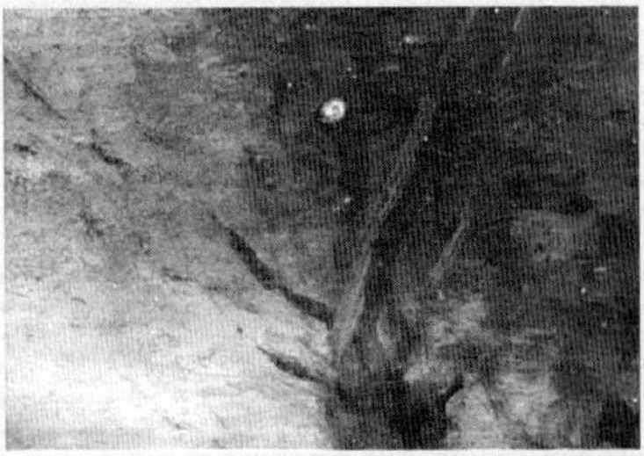

This detail, depicting a white spot, shows how a visible fault in an area of the painting can be explained by a combination of radiography and microscopic examination.

Radiography is a very important tool in the detection of forgeries. It brings to light evidence the forgers do not always think about concealing and provides information on the creative processes of the artist. It makes it possible to compare the physical elements of a particular picture with what is known, in this instance, about Corot's work and technique.

Macrophotography can establish the authenticity of a signature with near certainty. The problem can be more complicated if the painting is an early picture reworked several years later and signed at the same time or even later.

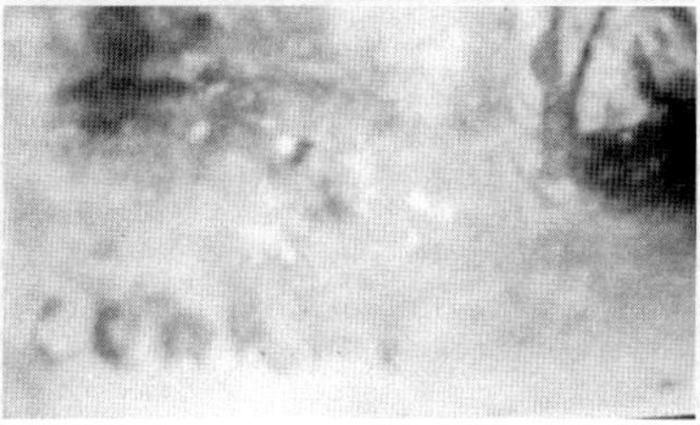

Reflectography (infrared examination) shows the presence of two signatures. The first is hardly visible, but a subsequent examination under the microscope definitely shows the name "Carot". This is, indeed, the name of a painter (perhaps one of Corot's entourage) who is cited by Alfred Robaut in the manuscript notes kept at the Bibliothèque nationale (a sort of fifth complementary volume to the *Catalogue raisonné*, concentrating on forgeries and never published).

picture, is due to a fault in the weft of the canvas.

The making of a painting

The glue used to mount the canvas onto the wood panel hinders the legibility of the radiography. But aside from the large gap (the black zone) in the center of the bottom edge of the painting, it is possible to make out an important technical detail: the major outlines of the composition and the details were painted during the same work sessions. It could be suspected, therefore, that the small figure in the foreground was added to the picture later to make the work "a true Corot."

Reflectography under infrared light is the final examination. This technique, which is much more powerful than infrared photography, allows the researcher to "see" beneath the color and to distinguish certain details that have been drawn directly onto the canvas. In this example, it shows the existence of two signatures (which is not unusual for Corot), only one of which appears to the naked eye. A very detailed comparison of this signature with authentic examples clearly demonstrates that it is a forgery.

The decision

Taking into account all the information gathered during the various research stages described above, a final conclusion is made after a series of

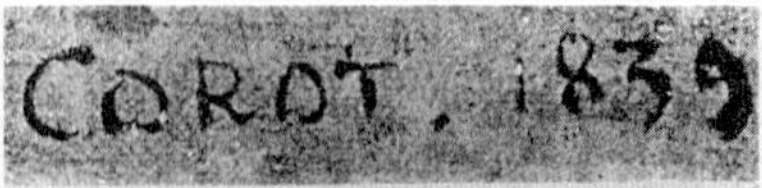

1839. — (*Œ. N° 397.*)

Vers 1850-55. — (*Œ. N° 1060.*)

Vers 1865-68. — (*Œ. N° 1626.*)

1874. — (*Œ. N° 2129.*)

Using examples of authentic signatures to make a comparison, researchers can dismiss faked signatures and more importantly, group together the "schools" or "studios" of forgers. The ones above date from 1833 to 1874 and were published in 1905 by Alfred Robaut.

comparisons with authentic works and other forgeries.

In this case, the doubts (aesthetic, signature, provenance), which were revealed by the naked eye, have been confirmed by the various physical examinations and research; the picture cannot be attributed to Corot. It is, however, a sufficiently honest treatment to make it attributable to one of Corot's many followers. An unknown person probably scratched off the signature of the first painter and replaced it with that of Corot, thereby increasing the market value of the picture, but it does not alter the natural charm of the work. Ultimately, this is all that matters, so long as the price is right.

Although this example did not include a pigment test, it shows that a systematic analysis of this type of picture and of authentic works by Corot should in the end enable us to establish a detailed chronological typology which will help art experts and museum curators assess the dozens of dubious paintings that appear on the market

every year. The quality of objective analysis, the stabilization of the art market, the reputation and above all the beauty of Corot's work (and of many other painters) will benefit from this research.

Gérard de Wallens

Overall view of the picture without the frame: having weighed up the evidence, it is worth taking another look at the work. It is not a Corot, not even a bad one, but nevertheless, it is a pleasant picture, probably painted by one of the artist's numerous followers or by one of his companions in old age, when paintings featuring ponds were extremely popular.

SELECTED BIBLIOGRAPHY

Catalogue raisonné and supplements

Robaut, Alfred. *L'Œuvre de Corot par Alfred Robaut, catalogue raisonné et illustré, précédé de l'histoire de Corot et de ses œuvres par Étienne Moreau-Nélaton*. 4 vols. Paris, 1905.

Schœller, André and Jean Dieterle. *Corot. Premier Supplément à «l'Œuvre de Corot» par A. Robaut et É. Moreau-Nélaton*. Paris, 1948.

———. *Corot. Deuxième Supplément à «l'Œuvre de Corot» par A. Robaut et É. Moreau-Nélaton*. Paris, 1956.

Dieterle, Jean. *Corot. Troisième Supplément à «l'Œuvre de Corot» par A. Robaut et É. Moreau-Nélaton*. Paris, 1974.

Dieterle, Pierre and André Pacitti. *Corot. Quatrième Supplément à «l'Œuvre de Corot» par A. Robaut et É. Moreau-Nélaton*. Paris, 1992.

Recent books and articles

Bazin, Germain. *Corot*. 3rd ed. Paris: Hachette, 1973.

Clarke, Michael. *Corot and the Art of Landscape*. New York: Cross River Press, 1991.

Dresel, Dr. Ines. *Camille Corot. Landschaftzeichnungen*. Fribourg, 1993.

Galassi, Peter. *Corot in Italy: Open-Air Painting and the Classical Landscape Tradition*. New Haven (CT): Yale University Press, 1991.

Gale, Iain. *Corot*. London, 1994.

Hopp, G. "Une œuvre tardive de Camille Corot: Le moine au violoncelle," in *La Gazette des Beaux-Arts*, Paris (March 1990): 129–140.

Jullien, A. and R. Jullien. "Les Campagnes de Corot, au nord de Rome (1826–1829)," in *La Gazette des Beaux-Arts*, Paris (May–June 1982): 179–202.

———. "Corot dans les montagnes de la Sabine," in *La Gazette des Beaux-Arts*, Paris (1984): 179–197.

———. "Corot dans les Castelli Romani," in *La Gazette des Beaux-Arts*, Paris (October 1987): 109–130.

Leymarie, Jean. *Corot*. Translated from the French by Stuart Gilbert. Geneva: Skira; New York: Rizzoli, 1992.

Wallens, Gérard de. "La Problématique du faux chez Corot dans les paysages de synthèse franco-italiens. À propos d'un tableau inconnu," in *La Revue des Archéologues et Historiens d'Art de Louvain*, Louvain-La-Neuve XXV (1992).

Wismann (F. E.), "Corot's Hymn to the Sun," in *Elvehjem Museum of Art Bulletin*. University of Wisconsin, Madison, 1982–1983: 9–17.

Exhibition catalogues

Exhibition of Corot's work. At the École nationale des beaux-arts. Biographical notice, Paris, 1875.

Figures de Corot. Salon d'Automne, Paris, 1909.

Estampes et dessins de Corot. Bibliothèque nationale. Exhibition organized in collaboration with the Louvre Museum, Paris, 1931.

Corot. Musée de l'Orangerie, Paris, 1936 (catalogue edited by P. Jamot).

Corot 1796–1875. An Exhibition of His Paintings and Graphic Works. The Art Institute of Chicago, October 6–November 13, 1960.

Figures de Corot. Louvre Museum, Paris, June–September 1962 (catalogue edited by S. Béguin, M. Dreyfus-Bruhl and M.-T. Lemoyne de Forges).

Corot. An Exhibition of Paintings, Drawings and Prints. Edinburgh Festival Society, Edinburgh, August 14–September 12, 1965.

Hommage à Corot. Peintures et dessins des collections françaises. Musée de l'Orangerie, Paris, June 6–September 29, 1975 (catalogue edited by H. Toussaint).

Achille Etna Michallon (*Les dossiers du Musée du Louvre)*. Paris, 1994: 156–160 (catalogue edited by B. Lesage, V. Pomarède and C. Stefani).

Corot, le génie du trait. Bibliothèque nationale, Paris, 1996 (catalogue edited by C. Bouret).

Corot. Galeries Nationales du Grand Palais, Paris. National Gallery of Canada, Ottawa. The Metropolitan Museum of Art, New York. 1996–1997 (catalogue edited by M. Pantazzi, V. Pomarède et G. Tinterow).

LIST OF ILLUSTRATIONS

Key: ***a****=above;* ***b****=below;* ***c****=center;* ***l****=left;* ***r****=right;* ***o/c****=oil on canvas;* ***o/p/c****=oil on paper mounted on canvas*

Abbreviations: BN=Bibliothèque nationale; CNMHS=Caisse nationale des Monuments historiques et des Sites; DGA=Department of Graphic Arts; R.=Robaut

COVER

FRONT PAGES

CHAPTER I

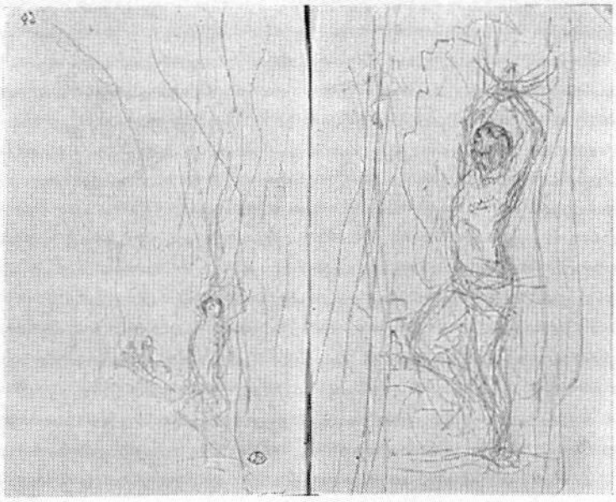

CHAPTER V

DOCUMENTS

INDEX OF COROT'S PAINTINGS

Page numbers in italics refer to captions and/or illustrations.

INDEX

Page numbers in italics refer to captions and/or illustrations.

COROT

PHOTOGRAPHIC CREDITS

AKG, Berlin/Paris 62a, 99r. All right reserved 97r, 130l, 130r, 131–132, 133a 134, 135al et b, 135ar, 143, 150ra, 150rb, 155. Archives photographiques, Caisse nationale des Monuments historiques et des Sites, Paris front cover, 115, 118b, 120, 122a. Art Center, Des Moines (IA) 112–113. The Art Institute, Chicago (IL) 73b, 117l. Artephot/Held, Paris 59b, 127l. Artephot/Ideca/Wildenstein Bros., Paris 112. Ashmolean Museum, Oxford 12, 30r. Bibliothèque nationale, Paris 13, 80–81, 95, 96–97, 99l, 100b, 101al, 101c, 101b, 110b, 156a, 156b. Bridgeman 76a, 114, 126. Jean-Loup Charmet, Paris 34–35, 37, 45bl, 89, 122–123, 142, 151a. Collection Debuisson, Paris 15. Private coll., 44. Private coll., London 38–39, 78–79. Private coll., New York (NY) 56. Private coll., Paris 108r. Private coll., Zürich 47a. Coll. Rau, France 118a. Coll. Dr. Marjorie Lewisohn, New York (NY) 66. Corcoran Gallery, Washington DC 3, 120–121. Église Saint-Nicolas-du-Chardonnet, Paris 97l. Galeria degli Uffizi, Firenze 52. Giraudon, Paris 9, 20a, 21, 22–23, 86–87, 133b, 136, 152, 157. Giraudon-Lauros, Paris 51b. Hugh Lane Municipal Gallery, Dublin 113. Institute of Art, Minneapolis (MN) 82. Kunsthalle, Bremen 16–17. Kunsthaus, Zürich 49. Kunstmuseum, Sankt Gallen 78l. Metropolitan Museum of Art, New York 59a, 67a, 80, 88–89, 116b. Minneapolis Institute of Art 117r. Musée d'Art et d'Histoire, Genève 38, 91a. Musée d'Art et d'Histoire, Metz 84–85. Museo d'Arte moderna, Venezia 19a. Musée d'Art, Saint-Lô 90–91. Musée dArt et d'Archéologie, Senlis 57. Musée départemental de l'Oise, © J.-L. Boutillier, Beauvais 28–29. Musée des Augustins, Toulouse 8, 106–107. Musée des Beaux-Arts, Lyon 122b. Musée des Beaux-Arts, Nantes 84. Musée du château de Versailles 109ar. Musée Mainssieux, Voiron 158. Musée municipal, Semur-en-Auxois 85. Museum of Art, Carnegie Institute, Pittsburgh (PA) 98l. Museum of Art, Philadelphia (PA) 60. Museum of Art, Providence (RI) 28, 91b. Museum of Fine Arts, Boston (MA) 43b, 64–65, 108l. National Galleries of Scotland, Edinburgh 31, 96. National Gallery of Art, Washington DC 123, 128, 129. National Gallery of Canada, Ottawa 50–51. Neue Pinakotek, München 1, 78r. Norton Simon Foundation, Pasadena (CA) 77. The Phillips Collection, Washington 40b. Photothèque des Musées de la Ville de Paris 62b, 109bl, 109br, 109al, 149. Réunion des Musées Nationaux front, back cover and spine, 2, 4–5, 6–7, 11, 14–15 18, 19b, 20b, 24–25, 26, 26–27, 27, 30l, 32, 33, 34, 36–37, 40a, 41, 42l, 43a, 45br, 46, 47b, 48, 50, 51a, 53, 54l, 54–55, 60–61, 61, 62–63, 67b, 68, 69l, 69r, 71, 72, 72/73, 73a, 74, 75a, 75b, 76b, 79, 81, 82–83a, 82–83b, 923, 93, 94, 98r, 100a, 101r, 102l, 102r, 103l, 103ra, 103rb, 104a, 105, 106l, 106r, 110a, 111, 115, 119, 124, 124–125, 125, 126–127, 127r, 137, 138, 141, 144, 145, 147, 150l, 151b, 154, 159 à 163, 164, 173. Archives Roger-Viollet, Paris 15b, 56–57, 88l, 88r. Shelburne Museum, Shelburne (VT) 118c, 121. Collection Sirot-Angel, Paris 45al et 45ar, 54r, 55, 58–59. Smith College Museum of Art, Northampton (MA) 70/71. Sterling and Francine Clark Institute, Williamstown (MA) 70. Taft Museum, Cincinnati (OH) 2, 104b. Wadsworth Atheneum, Hartford (MA) 58. Walters Art Gallery, Baltimore (MD) 42r.

ACKNOWLEDGMENTS

The authors and Éditions Gallimard would like to thank the following people for their assistance with this book: Claude Bouret, Department of Prints, Bibliothèque nationale; Bernadette Caille, Réunion des Musées Nationaux; Sylviane Dailleau, Photographic services, Bibliothèque nationale; Caroline Larroche; Monique Lepelley, Giraudon; Anne Norton, Metropolitan Museum of Art; Patricia Pomarède; Alexandra Rose, New York; Arlette Sérulaz, Department of Graphic Arts, Louvre Museum; Roger Van Schoute and Hélène Verourgstraete, University of Louvain; Anne de Wallens, Louvre Museum; Ruth Kozodoy, editorial department, Metropolitan Museum of Art; Sarah Burns, Harry N. Abrams, Inc.; Suzanne Bosmann; Caroline Sunderland for the translation of "Forgeries: true or false?"; and the private collectors who allowed their works to be reproduced, but chose to remain anonymous.

Vincent Pomarède is in charge of early nineteenth-century French painting (Romantic and Barbizon schools) in the Department of Painting of the Musée du Louvre, Paris. From 1988 to 1991, he was curator at the Restoration Service of the Musées de France. He has curated several exhibitions: "De Corot aux Impressionnistes" at the Grand Palais, Paris, in 1991, "Achille Etna Michallon" at the Musée du Louvre in 1994 and "Corot 1796–1875" at the Grand Palais in 1996; The National Gallery of Canada, Ottawa; and The Metropolitan Museum of Art, New York, 1996–1997.

Gérard de Wallens is an art historian at the University of Louvain in Belgium. Assistant curator of the "Corot 1796–1875" exhibition, he specializes in the study of forged Corot paintings, as well as in the study of the mutual influences between eighteenth-century French and Flemish painting. He recently wrote a book about Corot, published by Le Chêne/Somogy.

To Father Yves Delaunay, Chaplain at the Carmel de Lourdes.

EDITOR FOR THE ENGLISH VERSION: Jean Poderos

Distributed in 1996 by Gallimard

ISBN Gallimard 2–07–053379–4
ISBN Réunion des Musées nationaux
2–7118–3430–1
Printing number 76267

Printed in Evreux, France
by Kapp Lahure Jombart